SPELL ACROSS AMERICA

STORIES BY
KRIS HIRSCHMANN

ART BY
JAMES K. HINDLE

Roaring Brook Press
New York

Text copyright © 2017 by Roaring Brook Press
Illustrations copyright © 2017 by Roaring Brook Press
Published by Roaring Brook Press
Roaring Brook Press is a division of Holtzbrinck Publishing Holdings Limited Partnership
175 Fifth Avenue, New York, New York 10010
mackids.com
All rights reserved

Library of Congress Cataloging-in-Publication Data
Names: Hirschmann, Kris, 1967– author. | Hindle, James K., illustrator.
Title: Spell across America : 40 word-based stories, puzzles, and trivia facts
    offer a road-trip tour across the United States / Stories by Kris Hirschmann ;
    Illustrations by James K. Hindle.
Description: New York : Roaring Brook Press, 2017 | Series: Scripps National
    Spelling Bee | Includes index.
Identifiers: LCCN 2016035285 | ISBN 9781626721753 (hardcover)
Subjects: LCSH: English language—Orthography and spelling—Juvenile
    literature. | Short stories, American.
Classification: LCC PE1145.2 .H47 2017 | DDC 421/.52—dc23
LC record available at https://lccn.loc.gov/2016035285

Our books may be purchased in bulk for promotional, educational, or
business use. Please contact your local bookseller or the Macmillan Corporate
and Premium Sales Department at (800) 221-7945 ext. 5442 or by e-mail at
MacmillanSpecialMarkets@macmillan.com.

First edition, 2017
Book design by Andrew Arnold
Color separations by Embassy Graphics
Printed in China by Toppan Leefung Printing Ltd.,
Dongguan City, Guangdong Province

1 3 5 7 9 10 8 6 4 2

The Journey to the
★ Scripps National Spelling Bee ★

Victoria, TX

Fredericksburg, VA

Monroe, LA

Fort Worth, TX

★ Contents ★

★ Introduction ★

I love traveling with my family, whether we are near home or abroad, because it takes us out of our comfort zone, helps us appreciate other people and places, and brings us so much closer to one another. Among favorite adventures we've had: rafting in the Grand Canyon, climbing Mount Le Conte in the Great Smoky Mountains, wading up the Narrows in Zion National Park, and, closer to our home in Vermont, camping on islands in Lake Champlain and Green River Reservoir State Park.

Once, when my son was about six and we were driving through Colorado, he happily informed us: "Mama, Papa, I do scenery really well!" And he still does. When we hike, we all call my daughter "the machine" because she keeps up a steady, fast pace, focused on completing the hike while my wife and I stop to admire every rock, bird, or flower. It's just such a thrill to see baby otters in Yellowstone, mule deer in Rocky Mountain National Park, bats in a cavern in the Grand Canyon, or a possum in our own backyard. My wife loves wildflowers, the smaller the better: On our Mount Le Conte hike, we were thrilled to find over fifty species of wildflowers, some so small I wasn't sure they were flowers. Maybe we'll tackle making spore prints of mushrooms next. As for me, I'm the butt of way too many jokes involving how many thousands of photos I will have taken before we hit the first mile marker. But my family loves them later.

It's not all blissful: When things are going not so well, we jokingly call it "quality family time." On adventure after adventure, we find that even the downtime can be a boon. We always bring a deck of cards and play games. We stack the deck in favor of enjoyment with great snacks, we cook special but simple food, and we always try to bring along friends to share the experience, whether it's sitting in a lean-to until the rain stops, playing kayak-tag, or going up above the timberline on Vermont's beautiful signature mountain, Camel's Hump (which you can see on the state quarter). We learn so much about one another and grow so much closer by getting out into nature and exploring, whether we are going somewhere specific or just going out to see what we can see. And the words we learn while we're exploring—types of tiny wildflowers, adjectives to describe the scenery, names of animals, or new geological and geographical terms—we bring home with us and incorporate into our family's lexicon. They become words we use every day.

Next time you're on a road trip, take a look around. What do you see? What words can you bring back with you?

Happy travels, fellow word collectors!

Jacques A. Bailly

Dr. Jacques A. Bailly
Pronouncer for the Scripps National Spelling Bee
Associate Professor of Classics
1980 Scripps National Spelling Bee Champion

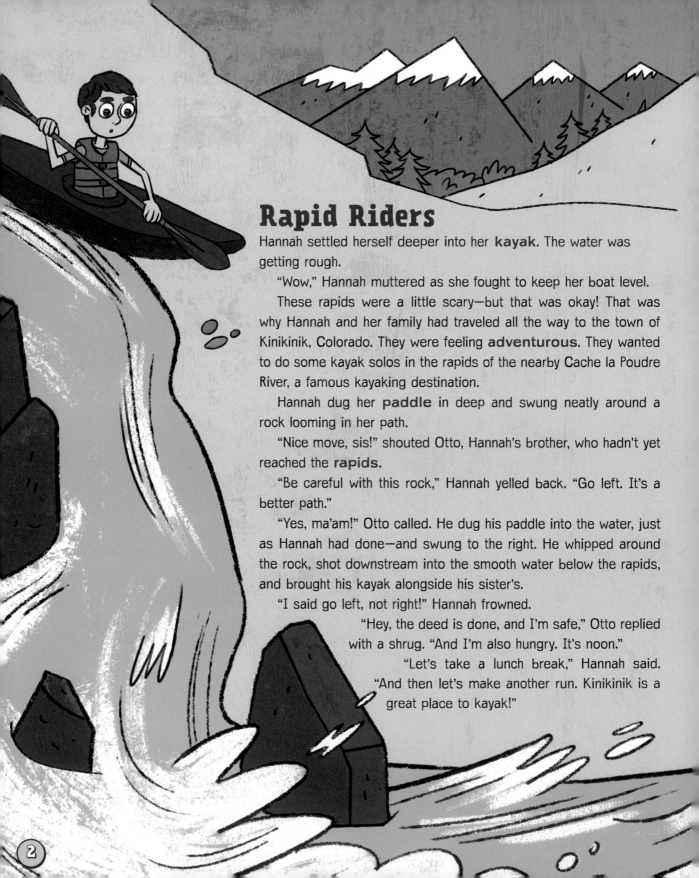

Rapid Riders

Hannah settled herself deeper into her **kayak**. The water was getting rough.

"Wow," Hannah muttered as she fought to keep her boat level.

These rapids were a little scary—but that was okay! That was why Hannah and her family had traveled all the way to the town of Kinikinik, Colorado. They were feeling **adventurous**. They wanted to do some kayak solos in the rapids of the nearby Cache la Poudre River, a famous kayaking destination.

Hannah dug her **paddle** in deep and swung neatly around a rock looming in her path.

"Nice move, sis!" shouted Otto, Hannah's brother, who hadn't yet reached the **rapids**.

"Be careful with this rock," Hannah yelled back. "Go left. It's a better path."

"Yes, ma'am!" Otto called. He dug his paddle into the water, just as Hannah had done—and swung to the right. He whipped around the rock, shot downstream into the smooth water below the rapids, and brought his kayak alongside his sister's.

"I said go left, not right!" Hannah frowned.

"Hey, the deed is done, and I'm safe," Otto replied with a shrug. "And I'm also hungry. It's noon."

"Let's take a lunch break," Hannah said. "And then let's make another run. Kinikinik is a great place to kayak!"

Spelling Words

kayak	KAHY-ak	*noun*	a long, narrow boat that you move with paddles
adventurous	ad-VEN-chuhr-uhs	*adjective*	not afraid to do new things
paddle	PAD-l	*noun*	a pole with a wide, flat part at the end used to move and steer small boats
rapids	RAP-idz	*plural noun*	parts of a river where the water is moving very quickly

★ Did You Know? ★

Other palindromic places in the United States include Ekalaka Lake (Montana), Oktahatko (Florida), Glenelg (Maryland), and Eleele (Hawaii).

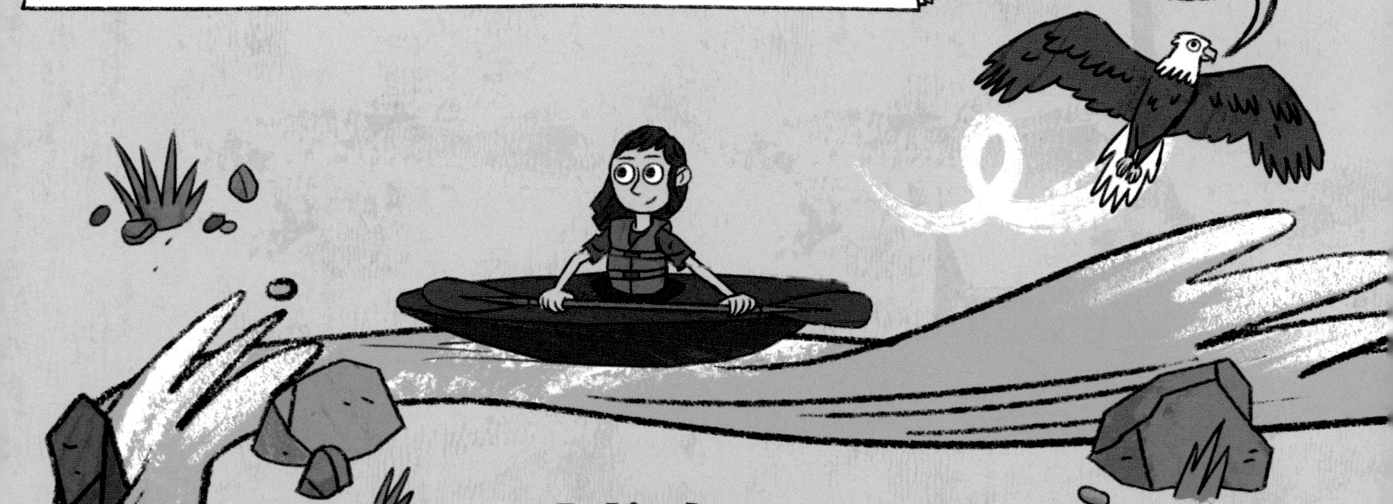

Palindromes

Palindromes are words or phrases that are spelled the same forward and backward. Single-word examples include *eye*, *stats*, and *refer*. Well-known palindromic phrases include *Madam, I'm Adam* and *A man, a plan, a canal: Panama.*

Not counting the words *a* and *I*, the story you just read includes eleven single-word palindromes. Can you spot all of them?

1. __________
2. __________
3. __________
4. __________
5. __________
6. __________
7. __________
8. __________
9. __________
10. __________
11. __________

Answers: Hannah, kayak, wow, level, Kinikinik, solos, sis, Otto, ma'am, deed, noon

Flying High

It is Super Secret Spelling Day, and Tim has decided to buy a **ticket** to the International Balloon Fiesta in the desert near Albuquerque, New Mexico. Tim sees hundreds of regular round balloons at the **festival**. He also sees balloons shaped like people, animals, plants, bugs, and objects. He wants to take photographs of these balloons, but today there is a special rule: Only shapes containing a certain letter may be photographed. Can you figure it out?

- ▸ He can photograph a cat, but not a dog.
- ▸ He can photograph a **cactus**, but not a flower.
- ▸ He can photograph a ladybug, but not a bee.
- ▸ He can photograph a castle, but not a house.
- ▸ He can photograph a villain, but not a **superhero**.
- ▸ He can photograph a bear, but not a frog.
- ▸ He can photograph an airplane, but not a bus.
- ▸ He can photograph a piñata, but not a clown.
- ▸ He can photograph a **roadrunner**, but not a penguin.
- ▸ He can photograph a shark, but not a sun.

So here is Tim's question: Can he photograph a balloon shaped like a pirate? Why or why not? What is the secret letter?

Answer: All of the shapes Tim can photograph contain the letter a. The word pirate has an a, so Tim can snap all the shots he wants! ARRRRR!

Vowels

The letter *a* is a vowel. There are five vowels in the English language: *a, e, i, o,* and *u.* The letter *y* also acts like a vowel sometimes. Vowels are called open sounds, which means they are made with an open airway.

These words are missing their vowels. Try using all five vowels, one by one, to complete each word. How many vowels work in each empty space?

1. b __ d
2. c __ t
3. n __ t
4. b __ g
5. t __ p

★ Did You Know? ★
Hot air balloons are large balloons filled with heated air, which makes them float in the sky. People can ride in baskets suspended beneath the balloons. At the nine-day-long Albuquerque International Balloon Fiesta, crowds gather each morning to watch over five hundred hot air balloons take off at once.

Spelling Words

ticket	TIK-it	*noun*	a piece of paper that lets you enter a show, go to an event, or travel in a vehicle
festival	FES-ti-vuhl	*noun*	an event where many people celebrate something together
cactus	KAK-tus	*noun*	a desert plant with fleshy stems and spines
superhero	SOO-per-heer-oh	*noun*	a character with amazing powers a human would not usually have
roadrunner	ROHD-run-er	*noun*	a desert bird that runs very fast

Answers: 1. bad, bed, bid, bod, bud; 2. cat, cot, cut; 3. net, nit, not, nut; 4. bag, beg, big, bog, bug; 5. tap, tip, top

Rock and Roll

"How long is this drive again?" Catherine asked her dad as she buckled herself into her seat.

"It depends on how we do it," Catherine's father replied. "If we go straight through, it's only about three hours from Nashville to Memphis."

"Ooh! Well, let's do that! I can't wait to get to Graceland," Catherine exclaimed. "Seeing Elvis Presley's **estate** will be the **experience** of a lifetime."

"Well, hold on a second. I'm excited, too, but I was thinking maybe we could spend a little more time on the drive," said Catherine's dad. "There are all kinds of cute little towns to explore along the way. We could stop in Waynesboro or Lexington for some real

down-home country food if you'd like to try some **barbecue**. Or we could check out the Southern **hospitality** in Summertown and Clarksburg. Who knows what we might find?"

"I guess you're right," Catherine said. "Enjoying the journey itself is the whole point of a road trip. It's not just an **expedition**, but also an opportunity to discover new things along the way."

"It is," Catherine's dad said. "But that doesn't mean we can't enjoy some old things, too. Crank up some Elvis music, kiddo. Let's rock while this car rolls!"

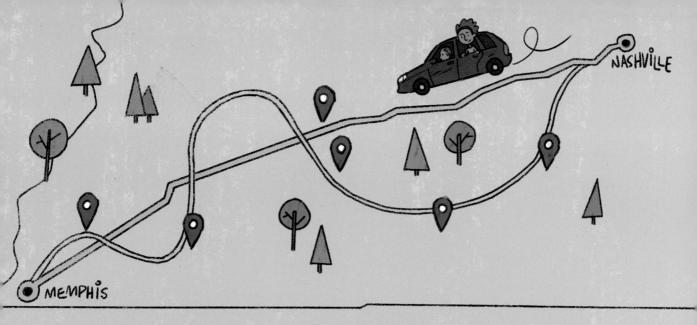

Place-Names

The names of many U.S. cities and places end in suffixes that mean "town" or otherwise suggest a place. The story you just read includes six examples: *-ville*, *-land*, *-boro*, *-ton*, *-town*, and *-burg*.

These well-known U.S. city names have been split apart! Match the beginnings with the correct suffixes to complete the words.

1. Washing_____   a. boro
2. Port_____   b. ville
3. Pitts_____   c. land
4. Louis_____   d. ton
5. Minnea_____   e. town
6. Greens_____   f. polis
7. James_____   g. burgh

> ★ **Did You Know?** ★
> There are a lot of names for the southern region of the United States, including Dixie, and just "The South."

Spelling Words

estate	i-STAYT	noun	a large house on a large property
experience	ik-SPEER-ee-uhns	noun	something you do or see
barbecue	BAHR-buh-kyoo	noun	food cooked on coals or a fire
hospitality	hahs-puh-TAL-uh-tee	noun	friendly treatment of guests
expedition	eks-puh-DISH-uhn	noun	a journey for a specific purpose

Come Sail Away

Colorful flags snapped in the wind as Olivia stepped onto the **pier**. She bounced with excitement as she walked. Olivia loved visiting the **marina** where her grandfather kept his sailboat. Sometimes she came just to help clean the boat, but today was even better. The weather was perfect for a ride on the wide-open waters of Lake Michigan.

"Ahoy, matey!" Olivia called as she reached her grandfather's **slip**.

"Welcome!" her grandfather replied, poking his head out of the boat's cabin. "You're right on time. I'm just setting up the **navigation** system."

"Is that like a **compass**?" Olivia asked.

"Sort of, but better," her grandfather said. "Compasses just show the cardinal directions—north, south, east, and west. A navigation system shows our exact position. That's very useful on the Great Lakes because they're so big! We could easily sail out of sight of land, if we wanted to. Even these tall buildings would disappear below the horizon." He waved his hand at the Chicago skyline looming over the marina.

"Well, I don't want to get lost—but I'd love to leave the city behind for a while," Olivia said with a smile.

"Me, too," her grandfather answered. "Hop on board. Let's go see what makes this lake so great!"

Word Origins, #1

Knowing a word's origin can help you understand how to spell it. The word *marina* was originally Spanish and Italian, meaning "shore" or "coast." In English, it has come to mean "a facility along the shore or coast where boats are docked."

The Spanish/Italian *marina* has even older origins. It comes from the Latin *marinus*, which means "sea." The English roots *mar-*, *mari-*, and *mer-* are related to this word.

Read these definitions. Can you figure out the *marinus*-related word that matches each definition?

1. A woman with a human torso and a fish tail   **m _ _ m _ i _**
2. Relating to the ocean   **m _ _ _ n _**
3. Another word for *sailor*   **m _ _ i _ _ r**
4. Relating to ocean commerce and navigation   **m _ _ _ t _ m _**
5. An area of wet, swampy land   **m _ _ s _**

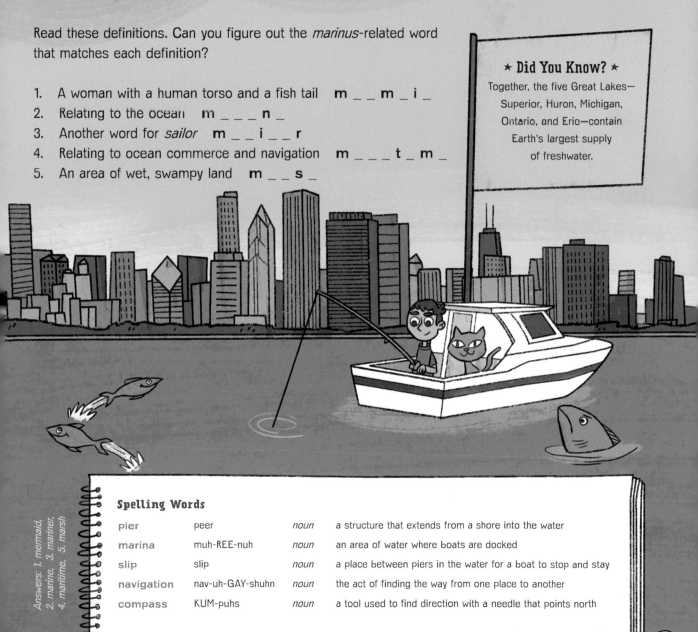

Answers: 1. mermaid, 2. marine, 3. mariner, 4. maritime, 5. marsh

Spelling Words

pier	peer	*noun*	a structure that extends from a shore into the water
marina	muh-REE-nuh	*noun*	an area of water where boats are docked
slip	slip	*noun*	a place between piers in the water for a boat to stop and stay
navigation	nav-uh-GAY-shuhn	*noun*	the act of finding the way from one place to another
compass	KUM-puhs	*noun*	a tool used to find direction with a needle that points north

Remember the Alamo

Rachel was having the time of her life visiting the Alamo, the site of a long-ago battle in Texas. She and her brother, Adam, had studied the site in school. Now they were seeing it with (their, thier) own eyes.

"Let's reenact the famous (seige, siege) of 1836," Adam called. "You be an American (soldeir, soldier). I'll be on the Mexican side."

"Okay," Rachel said. She moved next to the building.

"Go away, you (foreign, foriegn) invaders!" she shouted. "The people of Texas demand **independence** from Mexico. This is our (fronteir, frontier), not yours. We will never (yeild, yield)."

"Yes, you will!" Adam shouted back. "You'd better (beleive, believe) it! You only have two hundred men. We have thousands. Tell your commander in (cheif, chief) to **surrender**."

"Never," Rachel declared. "He will make this plain into a (battlefeild, battlefield) first."

"You won't go (queitly, quietly)?" Adam responded. "So be it. Prepare to (receive, recieve) a thrashing. We will (seize, sieze) this fort."

Adam rushed forward, waving his arms and shouting. Rachel ran to meet her brother. "Remember the Alamo!" she (creid, cried) as she ran.

When Rachel and Adam reached each other, they stopped and scowled for a moment. Then they burst out laughing.

"That was awesome," Rachel said between fits of giggles. "I never knew history could be so much fun. This Alamo trip is one **memory** I'll never forget!"

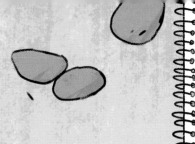

ie versus *ei*

It can be tricky to remember which words are spelled with *ie* and which are spelled with *ei*. There is a famous rule that says, "*I* before *e* except after *c*." This is true in many cases (for instance, *deceive*, *receipt*) but not always (*ancient*, *financier*). To be really good at *ie* and *ei*, you have to memorize many words.

The following word search puzzle contains the correctly spelled *ie* and *ei* words from the story. Find all thirteen words. Remember, if you can't find a word, you might be spelling it incorrectly.

```
F Y L T E I U Q Z F B
R E R I E H T Q C A N
O V F E I H C R T S R
N E H Z C P I T R Q D
T I B I T E L E W F C
I L X E D E I W Y Y U
E E X S F D X V I P Z
R B V I L H E G E I S
G J E O B F G Z L I E
B L S K C Y T F D H Q
D K N G I E R O F V N
```

★ Did You Know? ★
The Alamo complex covers 4.2 acres and includes several historic buildings. Now a tourist attraction, the famous site is located in San Antonio, Texas.

Search for the correct spelling of each word:

1. their, thier
2. seige, siege
3. soldeir, soldier
4. foreign, foriegn
5. fronteir, frontier

6. yeild, yield
7. beleive, believe
8. cheif, chief
9. battlefeild, battlefield
10. queitly, quietly

11. receive, recieve
12. seize, sieze
13. creid, cried

Seeing Stars

Erika thought this might be the best day of her life. Months ago, she had entered a contest in a magazine. The prize was two passes to attend a movie premiere in California—and Erika had won the jackpot! Now here she was on Hollywood Boulevard with her best friend, Rylee, waiting in line to enter the world-famous TCL Chinese Theatre, originally known as Grauman's Chinese Theatre.

"Do you think we'll see any stars?" Erika asked Rylee.

Just then, a cheer went up from the crowd. Craning her neck, Erika saw a limousine stopping in front of the theater. A well-dressed woman stepped out and waved to the crowd.

"Who's that?" said Rylee. "She's certainly glamorous, but I don't recognize her."

"That's the director," Erika answered. "Her job is telling the actors what to do."

At that moment, another limousine pulled up. Out stepped a dapper man.

"Ooh, he's important," Erika said. "That man runs the studio that paid to make the film."

Yet another limousine pulled up. The door opened . . . and out stepped Brad Rhodes, Erika's favorite celebrity of all time!

"OH. MY. GOSH!" Erika and Rylee squealed along with the rest of the crowd. "BRAD! WE LOVE YOU!"

Brad waved and disappeared into the theater. Erika and Rylee gave each other a high five.

"We got to see Brad Rhodes! And now we get to see a great film," Erika said with delight. "This is the best trip ever!"

Parts of Speech: Nouns

Knowing a word's part of speech and definition can help you spell the word.
A *noun* is a word that describes a person, a place, a thing, or an idea.

The story you just read contains six nouns from the *Spell Across America* Index
of Spelling Words (pages 84–86). Match each noun with its definition.

1. **premiere**   a. a person who supervises the filming of a movie and instructs the actors
2. **boulevard**   b. a famous person
3. **director**   c. a company that produces movies
4. **studio**   d. the first showing of a movie
5. **film**   e. a wide, important street
6. **celebrity**   f. a movie

★ **Did You Know?** ★
Nearly two hundred movie stars have left their handprints or footprints in the concrete in the forecourt of the TCL Chinese Theatre, otherwise known as Grauman's Chinese Theatre.

Spelling Words

jackpot	JAK-paht	*noun*	an impressive reward or prize
limousine	LIM-uh-zeen	*noun*	a large car driven by a professional driver
glamorous	GLAM-uh-ruhs	*adjective*	exciting and attractive
dapper	DAP-er	*adjective*	dressed in nice, stylish clothes

Answers: 1. d, 2. e, 3. a, 4. c, 5. f, 6. b

Busted Bell

"'The Liberty Bell is a historic symbol of our nation's freedom,'" Mona read aloud from the guidebook she was holding. "'It has rested in Philadelphia, also known as the birthplace of America, since colonial times.'" She lifted her eyes and gazed with interest at the bell hanging before her.

Mona's little brother, Raymond, didn't seem very impressed. He just snorted. "What's so great about an old bell? It's cracked," he said.

"I heard once that this BELL is famous because it broke during a celebration hundreds of years ago," Mona's father explained. "Someone gave it an extra-hard BELT. They wanted it to ring the loudest and BEST of all the bells in town. But they rang it so hard they made it BUST."

Mona frowned as she read further in the guidebook.

"Actually, Dad, it says here that no one knows for sure. Lots of people think the crack was spontaneous. It just happened for no reason," she said.

"Huh! Is that so? Well, I guess I learned something new today," Mona's dad replied. "But one thing is for sure—whatever made that BELL BUST, it created a national treasure. In my humble opinion, the Liberty Bell is definitely all it's cracked up to be!"

Word Ladders, #1

Word ladders are a type of spelling puzzle. You start with a word and change one letter at a time to make a different word. Mona's father made a word ladder to change the word BELL into BUST. Here is the word ladder:

BELL – BELT – BEST – BUST

Can you complete these easy word ladders? (Hint: Sometimes there is more than one way to complete a word ladder. If you find a different path than the one given in the answer key, that's fine.)

1.   **CAR – _ _ _ – VAN**
2.   **BOX – _ _ _ – BAG**
3.   **JET – _ _ _ – JOG**

Spelling Words

historic	hi-STOHR-ik	*adjective*	famous or important in the past
guidebook	GAHYD-book	*noun*	a book of information for tourists
colonial	kuh-LOH-nee-uhl	*adjective*	related to the original thirteen U.S. colonies
spontaneous	spahn-TAYN-ee-uhs	*adjective*	not planned or with little planning
national	NASH-uh-nuhl	*adjective*	relating to an entire country

Just Plain Great

The **suitcases** were packed, the car was full of **gasoline**, and everyone was ready to go! Noah and his family were driving from their home in Missouri to visit cousins in Colorado. It was a long trip, but Noah was excited. He had never been outside his home state.

"Tell me about the drive," he said to his mother.

"It's pretty," Noah's mother replied. "We'll get on **Interstate** 70 and head west. We'll drive all the way across Kansas. You'll get to see the Great **Plains**."

"Really? How many?" Noah asked.

"They stretch all the way across the state," his mother answered.

"Wow!" exclaimed Noah. "That's so cool! That must be thousands and thousands of airplanes!"

Noah's mother began to laugh. "Not P-L-A-N-E-S, Noah," she said. "Sorry to disappoint you. I meant P-L-A-I-N-S. The Great Plains are a big, flat region covered with **prairies** and grasslands."

"Oh," said Noah. "I would've liked to see thousands of P-L-A-N-E-S, but the P-L-A-I-N-S sound pretty interesting, too."

"They are," his mother agreed. "We'll see lots of farms, buffalo, and wildflowers. And we'll be at your cousins' house before you know it."

"That's just PLAIN great," Noah replied. "Colorado, here we come!"

Spelling Words

suitcase	SOOT-kays	*noun*	a container used to carry clothes and belongings when traveling
gasoline	GAS-uh-leen	*noun*	a liquid used as engine fuel
interstate	IN-tuhr-stayt	*noun*	an expressway connecting different states
plain	playn	*noun*	a large area of flat open land
prairie	PRAY-ree	*noun*	a meadow

★ Did You Know? ★

The Great Plains region covers about one-third of the United States. It includes part or all of ten states: Colorado, Kansas, Montana, Nebraska, New Mexico, North Dakota, Oklahoma, South Dakota, Texas, and Wyoming.

Homonyms

Words that sound alike but have different meanings are called homonyms. (They can also be called homophones, if they have the same spellings, but the Scripps National Spelling Bee still refers to them as homonyms.) In this story, the words *plains* and *planes* are homonyms. Even though these words are not spelled the same way, they sound exactly alike.

The following six words also appeared in this story. Can you think of a homonym for each one? Spell each homonym out loud.

1. **great**
2. **to**
3. **road**
4. **see**
5. **you**
6. **know**

Answers: 1. grate, 2. two/too, 3. rode, 4. sea, 5. ewe, 6. no

Take the Plunge

Sydney stared, awestruck, at the massive stream of water plunging into the depths below.

"This waterfall is incredible. I can see why Niagara Falls is such a big attraction," she said.

"There are actually three waterfalls that make up Niagara," Sydney's father replied. "Right now you're looking at American Falls and Bridal Veil Falls, and they're the small ones. Horseshoe Falls is the biggie."

"Can we visit that one, too?" asked Sydney.

"Sure," said her father. "But it's mostly on the Canadian side of the border, so we'll have to cross over."

"Did you bring our **passports**?" Sydney said.

"Yep," replied Sydney's dad. "We'll pop over there and see the falls. There's also a **boardwalk** on the Canadian side that leads to the site of a big **whirlpool**. We can check it out."

"Cool!" said Sydney. "And maybe I can buy a **postcard** to send to my classmates back home."

"Absolutely!" her father said with a smile. "But we'll get it at the end of our walk. Postcards aren't waterproof, and it's pretty damp around here from the waterfall's **mist**."

"Good plan," said Sydney. "I don't want my postcard to get ruined. I want to tell everyone about our amazing weekend adventure!"

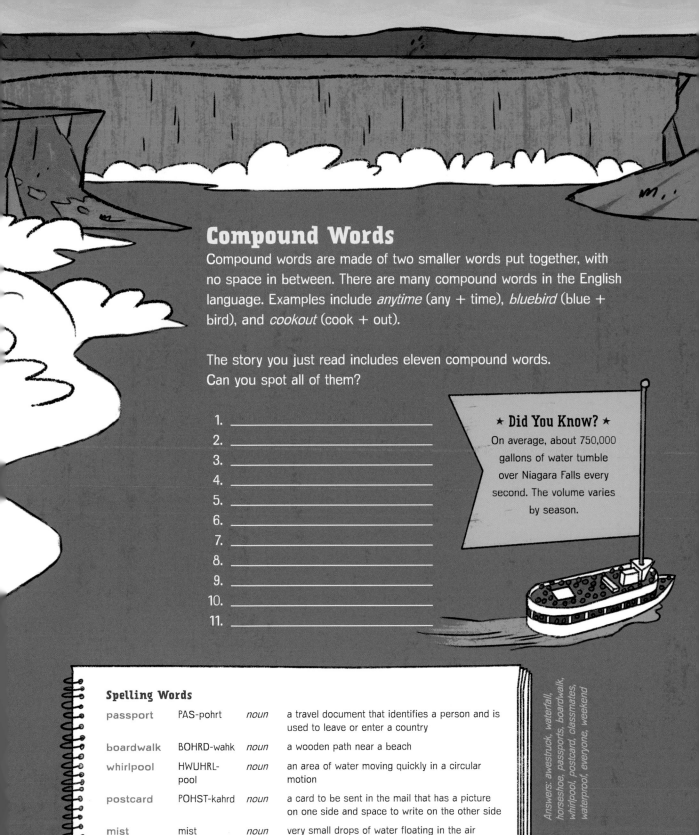

Compound Words

Compound words are made of two smaller words put together, with no space in between. There are many compound words in the English language. Examples include *anytime* (any + time), *bluebird* (blue + bird), and *cookout* (cook + out).

The story you just read includes eleven compound words. Can you spot all of them?

1. _____
2. _____
3. _____
4. _____
5. _____
6. _____
7. _____
8. _____
9. _____
10. _____
11. _____

★ **Did You Know?** ★

On average, about 750,000 gallons of water tumble over Niagara Falls every second. The volume varies by season.

Spelling Words

passport	PAS-pohrt	*noun*	a travel document that identifies a person and is used to leave or enter a country
boardwalk	BOHRD-wahk	*noun*	a wooden path near a beach
whirlpool	HWUHRL-pool	*noun*	an area of water moving quickly in a circular motion
postcard	POHST-kahrd	*noun*	a card to be sent in the mail that has a picture on one side and space to write on the other side
mist	mist	*noun*	very small drops of water floating in the air

Take a Hike

It's Super Secret Spelling Day again, and it's a big day for Soraya and Jill! The best friends are setting out to **backpack** the **Appalachian Trail**. They'll start their **trek** in Maine, where the trail begins, and head south. They will spend months walking 2,190 miles through fourteen states to reach the trail's end, in Georgia.

Or will they? At the trailhead, Soraya and Jill learn that they can only hike through states containing a certain letter. This is how their journey will look:

- ▶ Skip Maine
- ▶ Hike through New Hampshire
- ▶ Hike through Vermont
- ▶ Skip Massachusetts
- ▶ Skip Connecticut
- ▶ Hike through New York
- ▶ Hike through New Jersey
- ▶ Skip Pennsylvania
- ▶ Hike through Maryland
- ▶ Hike through West Virginia
- ▶ Hike through Virginia
- ▶ Skip Tennessee
- ▶ Hike through North Carolina

Soraya and Jill need to know one thing: Can they reach their **destination** at the trail's end in Georgia? What do you think? What is the secret letter?

Spelling Words

backpack	BAK-pak	*verb*	to travel or hike while carrying your belongings in a bag on your back
Appalachian	ap-uh-LAY-shuhn	*adjective*	related to the mountains of the same name
trail	trayl	*noun*	a path through a forest
trek	trek	*noun*	a very far walk
destination	des-tuh-NAY-shuhn	*noun*	the place where you are going

"R" We There Yet?

The names of twenty-one U.S. states contain the letter *r*. How many of them can you name? Try it! Then look at the list on this page to see which ones you missed. (Hint: The story gives you a head start. It names nine of these states that contain the letter *r*.)

Answer: U.S. states that contain the letter *r* are: 1. Arizona, 2. Arkansas, 3. California, 4. Colorado, 5. Delaware, 6. Florida, 7. Georgia, 8. Maryland, 9. Missouri, 10. Nebraska, 11. New Hampshire, 12. New Jersey, 13. New York, 14. North Carolina, 15. North Dakota, 16. Oregon, 17. Rhode Island, 18. South Carolina, 19. Vermont, 20. Virginia, 21. West Virginia

A Big Fan of the Everglades

The huge fan at the rear of the airboat whirred to life as the vessel pulled away from the dock.

"Hang on, folks," called the boat captain. "It's going to be a bumpy ride."

"Bring it on!" shouted Carla. "I like it bouncy. The bumpier, the better!"

Carla grinned as the boat picked up speed. The breeze felt good against her sweaty forehead. The Florida Everglades sure were sunny—and hot!

The fan roared as the boat skipped across the water's swampy surface, racing toward a bank of leafy mangroves. The boat slowed as it entered a shady tunnel in the vegetation.

"Keep your eyes peeled for alligators," the captain announced. "Shouldn't be too tough to spot them. Those scaly critters are everywhere in these parts. Remember, hands in the boat! Your fingers look tasty to a gator."

Carla peered into a clearing between the mangrove trees. Sure enough, she spotted a pair of beady eyes staring back at her.

"I see one!" she shrieked. She pointed out the gator to the other passengers.

"Nice job!" said the captain. "Now let's skedaddle. It's getting cloudy, and we should head back before it gets rainy. Hold on to your hats, because we're going even faster this time. It's about to get windy around here!"

-y Endings

Adding the letter *y* to the end of a word can change a noun or a verb into an adjective. For instance, the noun *sleep* changes to the adjective *sleepy*. The verb *jump* changes to the adjective *jumpy.*

There are a few rules for adding the -*y* ending. There are exceptions to these rules, but in general:

a. If a word ends with two or more consonants, just add *y*.
b. If a word ends with one consonant preceded by two vowels, just add *y*.
c. If a word ends with one consonant preceded by one vowel, double the final consonant before adding the *y*.
d. If a word ends with a silent *e*, drop the *e* before adding the *y*.

Look at the list of -*y* adjectives from the story you just read. Put the letter of the spelling rule that applies to each word in the space.

	Word	Rule (a, b, c, d)			Word	Rule (a, b, c, d)
1.	bumpy	_____		8.	scaly	_____
2.	bouncy	_____		9.	tasty	_____
3.	sweaty	_____		10.	beady	_____
4.	sunny	_____		11.	cloudy	_____
5.	swampy	_____		12.	rainy	_____
6.	leafy	_____		13.	windy	_____
7.	shady	_____				

★ **Did You Know?** ★
The Everglades region is often described as a swamp. But the water is actually a huge, slow-flowing river!

Spelling Words

airboat	AYR-boht	*noun*	a boat that moves using an airplane propeller and rudder
swampy	SWAHMP-ee	*adjective*	related to land that is always wet
mangrove	MANG-rohv	*noun*	a tropical tree with roots that grow from its branches into swamps
alligator	AL-uh-gayt-er	*noun*	a large, long reptile with thick skin, sharp teeth, and a long, tapering head
clearing	KLEER-ing	*noun*	an open area of land without trees

Answers: 1. a, 2. d, 3. b, 4. c, 5. a, 6. b, 7. d, 8. d, 9. d, 10. b, 11. b, 12. b, 13. a

The Museum of Modern Art

Taxi Trouble

After a long day exploring the **Museum** of Modern Art in New York City, Sergio and his mother were beat. They were ready to hail a **taxi** and head back to their **hotel**.

The pair walked out of the museum and stood by the street. They saw a cab approaching.

"Taxi!" shouted Sergio, holding out his arm. But the cab didn't stop. It zoomed right on by.

Another cab approached. Sergio stuck out his arm again. "Taxi!" he shouted, louder this time. But this cab didn't stop either.

"What's going on here?" he wondered out loud.

A nearby man started laughing. "Sorry, I don't mean to be rude," he said. "You're tourists, right?"

"Yes, we are," Sergio replied.

"I can tell. Only the taxis with the numbers on top of their cars lit up are accepting passengers. Those without their numbers lit or with 'off-duty'

signs are already full, and it's difficult to get a taxi at this time of day in New York. Why don't you try a different type of **transportation**? You can take the train or a bus."

"Just one more try," Sergio said, gritting his teeth. He thrust his arm into the air for a third time.

"TAXI!" he hollered loudly at an approaching cab, this time one that had its numbers lit up . . . and the car came screeching to a halt!

"Huh. Beginner's luck," said the man with a smile. "Well done."

"Thanks," answered Sergio as he and his mother scrambled into the car. "We'll definitely follow your suggestions . . . tomorrow. Right now we need to get off our aching feet!"

Word Origins, #2

Knowing a word's origin can help you understand how to spell it. The word *taxi* is an abbreviation of the closely related German and French words *Taxameter* and *taximètre*. Both words mean "a device to record distance and fare." These words in turn are related to the Latin word *taxare*, which means "to tax or charge."

Read these definitions. Can you figure out the *tax*-related word that matches each definition?

1. A fee on goods or services paid to the government   t _ _
2. Someone who pays these government fees   t _ _ p _ _ _ _
3. A job or duty   t _ s _
4. What an airplane driving on the runway is doing   t _ _ i _ _ g
5. The full name for a taxi   t _ _ _ c _ _

★ **Did You Know?** ★
A typical New York taxi travels 70,000 miles per year —that's roughly the same as circling Earth 2.8 times!

Spelling Words

museum	myoo-ZEE-um	*noun*	a building where collections of interesting items are displayed
taxi	TAK-see	*noun*	a car that you can hire to take you somewhere
hotel	hoh-TEL	*noun*	a building that rents rooms for people to stay in while traveling
transportation	tranz-pohr-TAY-shuhn	*noun*	a way of traveling

Confusing Cruise

Harper couldn't wait for summer to arrive! She and her family were going on the vacation of a lifetime—a three-week paddleboat **cruise** up the (Missisippi, Mississippi) River. The boat would leave from the river's southern end near the **Gulf** of Mexico and travel north through ten states.

Harper thought she must have looked at the cruise **itinerary** a hundred times already. But she couldn't resist reading it yet again.

"'Your adventure begins in New Orleans, where passengers will board the boat and find their cabins. The ship will then **embark** on its **voyage**,'" Harper read out loud. "'Over the next three weeks, you will move through or alongside the states of (Louisiana, Louisianna), (Missisippi, Mississippi), (Arkansaw, Arkansas), (Tennessee, Tenessee), (Kentucky, Kintucky), (Missouri, Missourri), (Illinnois, Illinois), (Iowah, Iowa), and (Wisconsin, Wisconnsin) before reaching the final state, (Minesota, Minnesota). Here, you will disembark with a lifetime's worth of wonderful memories.'"

"I'm sure the memories *will* be wonderful," said Harper's mom, who had just walked into the room. "But let's talk about your *spelling* memory! Do you think you could spell all those states' names without seeing them written down?"

"I don't know," Harper confessed. "Some of them are pretty confusing. But I bet I'll have them nailed down after I read the itinerary *another* hundred times. All I know for sure is that summer can't get here soon enough!"

Spelling Words

cruise	krooz	*noun*	a vacation with multiple stops taken on a boat
gulf	guhlf	*noun*	a large part of an ocean that is partly surrounded by land
itinerary	ahy-TIN-uhr-ayr-ee	*noun*	a list of the places you will go on a trip
embark	em-BAHRK	*verb*	to start a journey
voyage	VOI-ij	*noun*	a long trip

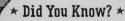

★ **Did You Know?** ★
The Mississippi River is about 2,500 miles long and up to 11 miles wide in some places.

State Names

U.S. state names can be very hard to spell. The names have different origins in many different languages, and they do not always follow the rules of English spelling. The only way to get them right is to memorize them.

The following word search puzzle contains the correctly spelled state names from the story. Find all ten names. Remember, if you can't find a name, you might be spelling it incorrectly.

```
K  V  A  T  O  S  E  N  N  I  M
E  K  E  E  S  S  E  N  N  E  T
N  N  I  L  L  I  N  O  I  S  U
T  I  H  D  P  J  Q  Q  N  B  F
U  S  U  S  A  N  A  K  R  A
C  N  J  D  K  S  S  A  U  O  U
K  O  I  R  U  O  S  S  I  M  Y
Y  C  H  W  I  C  F  G  W  B  T
T  S  A  N  A  I  S  I  O  U  L
M  I  S  S  I  S  S  I  P  P  I
V  W  M  D  M  W  G  A  W  O  I
```

Search for the correct spelling of each state name:

1. Louisiana, Louisianna
2. Missisippi, Mississippi
3. Arkansaw, Arkansas
4. Tennessee, Tenessee
5. Kentucky, Kintucky
6. Missouri, Mizzouri
7. Illinnois, Illinois
8. Iowah, Iowa
9. Wisconsin, Wisconnsin
10. Minesota, Minnesota

Answers: 1. Louisiana, 2. Mississippi, 3. Arkansas, 4. Tennessee, 5. Kentucky, 6. Missouri, 7. Illinois, 8. Iowa, 9. Wisconsin, 10. Minnesota

Sandy Stuff

Raul felt so lucky to live in Boston. Just over an hour ago, he had been sweating in a city apartment. Now he was wiggling his toes in the sand and watching seagulls fly overhead. It was great to live so close to Cape Cod's magnificent beaches!

"I am boiling hot! Are you ready to **plunge** into the water with me to cool down?" Raul's father asked.

"I don't know," Raul said hesitantly. "Those waves look pretty big."

"It's okay," Raul's father replied. "I'll stay near you. And the **local** lifeguards will help us if anything goes wrong."

"I know you're right, and I trust you. But for right now, I think I'll stay on **shore**," Raul said. "I want to make a few sand castles before I get into the water. And maybe the **surf** will die down a little bit in the meantime."

"Fair enough," said Raul's father. "Can I help with the sand castles?"

"You sure can!" Raul answered. "Let's grab the buckets and get to work. We'll get all sandy—and then I'll *definitely* be ready to swim!"

Spelling Words

plunge	plunj	*verb*	to jump suddenly from a high place
local	LOH-kuhl	*adjective*	relating to a particular place
shore	shohr	*noun*	the land next to a sea; the coast
surf	surf	*noun*	the large waves that hit the shore and make white foam

Parts of Speech: Plural Nouns

Knowing a word's part of speech and definition can help you spell the word.

A *plural noun* is a word that describes more than one person, place, thing, or idea.

The story you just read contains six plural nouns from the *Spell Across America* Index of Spelling Words (pages 84–86). Match each plural noun with its definition.

1.	**seagulls**	a.	sandy areas near an ocean or lake
2.	**beaches**	b.	open containers with handles
3.	**waves**	c.	workers whose jobs are to protect people who are swimming
4.	**lifeguards**	d.	small structures or buildings made from wet sand
5.	**sand castles**	e.	large gray-and-white birds found near beaches
6.	**buckets**	f.	areas of moving water that flow toward and away from the shore

Answers: 1. e, 2. a, 3. f, 4. c, 5. d, 6. b

Pass the Salt

Greg stood with a group of tourists on an overlook, gazing across Utah's Great Salt Lake.

"This thing is huge," he said in awe.

"It is," agreed the tour guide. "The lake's basin covers an area of over a million acres. It is the largest U.S. lake west of the Mississippi River. In fact, some people call it an inland sea. And guess what? The lake's water is salty, not fresh. This lake is at least three times saltier than the ocean!"

"Wow! How does a lake get all that salt?" Greg asked.

"Well, it's pretty simple," the guide said with a wink. "You start with any plain old LAKE." He pointed at the water.

"Next you MAKE a grand, magical gesture." The guide waved his arms.

"Now you make another one, just for the SAKE of it." He waved again.

"Okay. Now you hop into your car and drive to the nearest grocery store. Look for a SALE. Buy lots and lots of SALT, and bring it right back here. Then dump it into the lake. See? The LAKE is now full of SALT!"

Greg laughed.

"That's funny," he said. "Now, what's the real answer to my question?"

"Actually, the lake is full of salty minerals that collected over millions of years," the guide replied, smiling.

"That makes more sense," Greg replied. "It looks to me like the Great Salt Lake doesn't need any sales to be salty . . . or amazing!"

Word Ladders, #2

The tour guide made a word ladder to change the word LAKE into SALT.
Here is the word ladder:

LAKE – MAKE – SAKE – SALE – SALT

Can you complete these easy word ladders?

1. **SWIM** – _ _ _ _ – **SWAN**
2. **WEST** – _ _ _ _ – **NEAT**
3. **POND** – _ _ _ _ – **BAND**

★ Did You Know? ★
The Great Salt Lake has no fish! The salt level is too high for fish to survive.

Spelling Words

overlook	OH-vuhr-look	*noun*	a place with a beautiful view of the area below
basin	BAY-sin	*noun*	a depression in the surface of the land
acre	AY-ker	*noun*	a unit of land area (4,840 square yards)
inland	IN-land	*adjective*	related to the part of the country away from the coast
minerals	MIN-uh-ruhlz	*plural noun*	substances (like stones or coal) that are formed in the ground and are not animal or vegetable

A Beautiful View

Reina looked at the **breathtaking** scenery whizzing by outside the car window. She and her family were on a cross-country road trip. Right now they were driving near the Arizona-Utah **border**. Everything was **desert**, desert, desert, as far as the eye could see.

But wait! Something different was looming on the horizon—something big. It was sort of like a mountain, but bare, brownish red, and rocky. It was jagged, with an oddly squared-off top. It didn't look like any mountain Reina had ever seen.

"What is *that*?" she asked.

"*That* is something special," Reina's father replied. "We just entered Monument **Valley**, and that is a **butte**."

"Yes, it certainly is pretty!" Reina answered. "But what is it?"

"A butte," her father repeated, puzzled.

"No, no. You already told me it's beautiful. I want to know its proper name," Reina said.

"Aha! I get it!" Reina's father said. "I didn't mean it was a B-E-A-U-T, like a beauty. It's a rock formation that sticks up from a plain, and it's spelled B-U-T-T-E. It sounds just like *beaut*, so I can see why you were confused."

Reina giggled. "Me, too," she said. "But now I get it. I hope we see lots more of these BUTTES on our drive. They're BEAUTS, for sure!"

Clipping Words

The word *beaut*, used as a noun, is an abbreviated form of the noun *beauty*. It is made by keeping one syllable of the original word and dropping the rest. This is sometimes called "clipping" because one part of the word is "clipped" off.

Here are some other words that are often clipped to just one syllable. Can you figure out the shortened form of each word?

1. radical
2. doctor
3. maximum
4. picture
5. representative
6. trigonometry
7. champion
8. advertisement

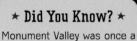

★ Did You Know? ★
Monument Valley was once a high, flat plateau. Over millions of years, wind and water carved the land into the formations we see today.

Spelling Words

breathtaking	BRETH-tay-king	*adjective*	very exciting
border	BOHR-duhr	*noun*	an edge
desert	DEH-zuhrt	*noun*	a dry area of land with few plants and very little rain
valley	VAL-ee	*noun*	a low area of land between mountains
butte	byoot	*noun*	a hill with a flat top and steep sides

KABOOM! KABLAM!

The view from this observatory was great! Deshawn gazed across a barren expanse at a **panorama** of Mount St. Helens, a **volcano** in Washington State that had erupted violently in 1980.

"Tell me again what happened," Deshawn begged his aunt.

"Well, the ground started to rumble," she said. "Steam hissed out of the volcano's sides. The heat made lightning bolts crack across the sky. Officials knew something was brewing, so they declared a state of **emergency**."

"Were they right?" Deshawn asked.

"They sure were," his aunt replied. "On the morning of May 18, the whole top of the volcano blew off. People heard the **eruption**—which sounded like *Bang! Bang! Bang!*—from a distance of over a hundred miles away."

"It must have been *really* loud up close," Deshawn said.

"They say the eruption made an earsplitting *KABOOM*," Deshawn's aunt replied. "And it wasn't just loud. It was very damaging, too. It destroyed forests and homes for miles around."

"Could that ever happen again?" Deshawn squeaked nervously.

"Mount St. Helens is still active—so yes, it could," his aunt replied. "But scientists learned a lot from the 1980 eruption. They know what to look for now. This **observatory** is only open when conditions are safe, so we should be fine."

"Good!" exclaimed Deshawn. "In that case, I'm glad we're here. The volcano is really cool. In fact, my mind is officially blown—*KABLAM!*"

Onomatopoeia

Words that imitate sounds are known as onomatopoeia (ON-uh-MAH-tuh-PEE-uh). Examples of onomatopoeia include *moo*, *snort*, *ding-dong*, and *hiccup*.

The story you just read includes seven examples of onomatopoeia. Can you spot all of them?

1. _____
2. _____
3. _____
4. _____
5. _____
6. _____
7. _____

Answers: rumble, hissed, crack, Bang, KABOOM, squeaked, KABLAM

★ **Did You Know?** ★

The lateral blast from the 1980 Mount St. Helens eruption traveled at speeds of over 300 miles per hour and reached maximum temperatures of up to 660 degrees Fahrenheit.

Spelling Words

panorama	pan-uh-RAM-uh	*noun*	a wide view
volcano	vahl-KAY-noh	*noun*	a mountain with a hole in the top that sometimes erupts with lava
emergency	e-MUR-juhn-see	*noun*	an unexpected, dangerous, or negative situation
eruption	i-RUP-shun	*noun*	an explosion of rocks, ash, and lava
observatory	ub-ZER-vuh-toh-ree	*noun*	a building with equipment for the viewing of natural facts or events of interest to science

Ride 'Em, Cowboy

It's Super Secret Spelling Day again, and today also happens to be the **highlight** of Travis's entire year. It's the day of the world bull-riding competition at the Frontier Days festival in Travis's hometown of Cheyenne, Wyoming. Wyoming is the heart of America's **cowboy culture**, and the world's most **rugged** riders attend this **rodeo** each year. Travis loves trying to guess which ones will last eight whole seconds without getting bucked off.

Today only riders with a certain letter combination in their names have succeeded. So far Travis has watched twenty rides, and the results have gone like this:

- ▶ Connor succeeded, but Chuck failed.
- ▶ Tommy succeeded, but Tyler failed.
- ▶ Will succeeded, but Wes failed.
- ▶ Matt succeeded, but Marc failed.
- ▶ Warren succeeded, but Whit failed.
- ▶ Johnny succeeded, but Jake failed.
- ▶ Isaac succeeded, but Ian failed.
- ▶ Wyatt succeeded, but Wade failed.
- ▶ Jerry succeeded, but Josh failed.
- ▶ Cooper succeeded, but Chris failed.

Travis wonders how *he* would do at bull riding. Based on his name, do you think Travis would succeed or fail? What advice would you give him?

Double Letters

Double-letter names, like the ones in this story, aren't usually too tough to remember. But many other double-letter words can be tricky. They are often spelled incorrectly.

Look at this list. Fill in the blanks with the correct choice—a single letter or a double letter.

1. ba ___ oon (*l* or *ll*)
2. bro ___ oli (*c* or *cc*)
3. mi ___ pell (*s* or *ss*)
4. commi ___ ee (*t* or *tt*)
5. pas ___ ime (*t* or *tt*)

6. pre ___ er (*f* or *ff*)
7. roo ___ ate (*m* or *mm*)
8. unti ___ (*l* or *ll*)
9. va ___ uum (*c* or *cc*)
10. refe ___ ed (*r* or *rr*)

Spelling Words

Word	Pronunciation	Part of Speech	Definition
highlight	HAHY-lahyt	*noun*	one of the best parts of something
cowboy	KAU-boi	*noun*	a person who rides a horse on a ranch or in a rodeo
culture	KUHL-chuhr	*noun*	the ways of life in a particular area
rugged	RUHG-id	*adjective*	having a rough surface; rough and strong in character
rodeo	ROH-dee-oh	*noun*	a competition in horse riding, bull riding, roping animals, etc.

Answers: 1. balloon, 2. broccoli, 3. misspell, 4. committee, 5. pastime, 6. prefer, 7. roommate, 8. until, 9. vacuum, 10. referred

A "Ful" Day

WHOOSH!

Joon flinched as a **column** of boiling water blasted out of the ground a short distance in front of her.

"Right on time," shouted Joon's brother, Lee, checking his watch. "I guess that's why they call it Old Faithful."

"This **geyser** sure is powerful," Joon shouted back. "And beautiful, too."

Lee nodded as the water stream slowed, then stopped. "There are thousands of geysers here in Yellowstone National Park. Old Faithful isn't the biggest one, but it's the most famous," he said.

"It erupts at very regular **intervals**. The gap **averages** about ninety minutes. Rangers can predict the gap even more closely by timing each event. The longer an eruption, the longer the gap will be."

"That's very helpful information," said Joon.

"Yep. Old Faithful is thoughtful like that." Lee grinned. "It gives us time to do some other things before the next eruption."

"Sounds good," said Joon. "And to be truthful, I'm thankful for the break. I feel like we've walked all the way across Wyoming today. It's time to rest my feet!"

−ful Endings

Adding the suffix -ful usually changes a noun into an adjective: hope + ful = hopeful, harm + ful = harmful. The suffix is always spelled with just one l, not two. The resulting adjective means "full of [the root noun]." So something that is harmful is full of harm. Something that is hopeful is full of hope.

Look at the -ful adjectives from the story you just read. Separate the root noun in each word.

	Word	Root
1.	**faithful**	full of _____
2.	**powerful**	full of _____
3.	**beautiful**	full of _____
4.	**helpful**	full of _____
5.	**thoughtful**	full of _____
6.	**truthful**	full of _____
7.	**thankful**	full of _____

Just for fun: Try adding the suffix −less to each root noun to form an adjective that means "lacking [root noun]."

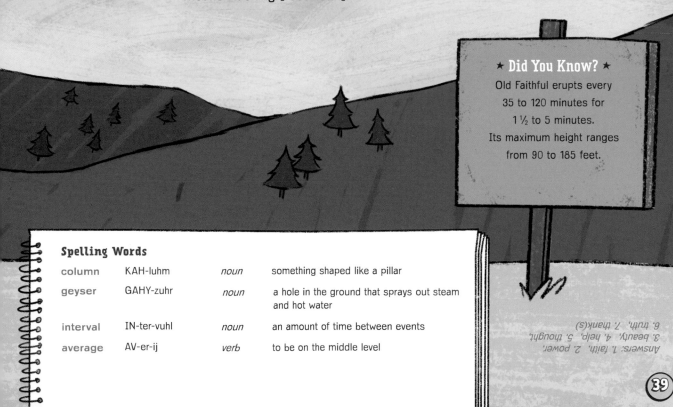

★ **Did You Know?** ★
Old Faithful erupts every
35 to 120 minutes for
1 ½ to 5 minutes.
Its maximum height ranges
from 90 to 185 feet.

Spelling Words

column	KAH-luhm	*noun*	something shaped like a pillar
geyser	GAHY-zuhr	*noun*	a hole in the ground that sprays out steam and hot water
interval	IN-ter-vuhl	*noun*	an amount of time between events
average	AV-er-ij	*verb*	to be on the middle level

Answers: 1. faith, 2. power,
3. beauty, 4. help, 5. thought,
6. truth, 7. thank(s)

Take a Deep Breath

"Let me put some sunscreen on your back," said Jackie's mother as the boat churned through the water off the coast of the Florida Keys. "You're about to be facedown in this blistering sunlight."

"Good idea," Jackie replied. "I don't want to get a sunburn while I snorkel. I might be in the water for hours. There's a lot to see on these coral reefs!"

"There sure is," said the boat captain, who was listening to his passengers' conversation. "The reef we're going to is famous for its pretty shells. You might find some fancy ones. Look out for jellyfish, though. They sting."

"Are there any sharks?" Jackie asked nervously.

"Oh, sometimes. But they're little and harmless around here. And besides, you'd look scary to a shark with that snorkel sticking out of your mouth," the captain replied.

"So a snorkel lets me breathe underwater and acts like shark repellant, too? Nifty." Jackie grinned.

"Yep!" said the captain. "And you know what else is nifty? We're right over the reef now—and there's not a shark in sight. Go ahead and jump in."

"Okay," said Jackie. "But even with my scary snorkel, I'm going to jump right back out if I see any creepy critters. I want to be around to enjoy Florida's coral reefs for many, many years to come!"

Word Origins, #3

Knowing a word's origin can help you understand how to spell it. The word *snorkel* comes from the German naval slang *Schnorchel*, which means "nose" or "snout." It referred to an air shaft for submarines. The current spelling was first used in English to mean "a curved breathing tube for swimmers" in 1951.

Read these definitions of English words with a German origin. Can you figure out the word that matches each definition?

1. A wiener dog   d _ _ _ s _ _ _ d
2. Polite response to a sneeze   G _ _ _ _ dh _ _ _
3. A slow, formal dance   w _ _ _ z
4. A small, stub-tailed rodent, often a pet   h _ _ _ t _ _
5. The school year before first grade   k _ _ _ _ _ g _ _ t _ _

Spelling Words

sunscreen	SUHN-skreen	*noun*	lotion you put on your skin to protect it from sunburn
coast	kohst	*noun*	the land near an ocean
snorkel	SNOHR-kuhl	*verb*	to use a hard rubber or plastic tube to breathe while moving facedown at or just below the surface of the water
shell	shel	*noun*	the hard protective covering of an animal or insect
jellyfish	JEL-ee-fish	*noun*	a soft marine creature with a body shaped like an umbrella and long tentacles

Answers: 1. dachshund, 2. Gesundheit, 3. waltz, 4. hamster, 5. kindergarten

License to Fish

Sunlight glinted off the Maine waters as the first lobster trap came to the (surface, surfase). Casey grinned as he watched a fisherman heave the trap over the railing. This fishing charter was so fun!

The deckhand plunged his gloved hand into the trap and pulled out a lobster.

"(Nice, Nise) one!" Casey exclaimed.

"Yep. It's a fine (specimen, spesimen)," the deckhand replied. "Here, kid. You hold it while I measure it."

Casey held the squirming shellfish gingerly while the deckhand grabbed a ruler.

"Why do you have to measure it?" he asked.

"If it's too small, we have to (releace, release) it," the deckhand replied. "And unfortunately, it looks like that's the (cace, case) here. This little guy is (cloce, close) to legal size, but not quite.

I measured it (twice, twise). If the marine (police, polise) stop us, I'll be in big trouble."

"Aw!" said Casey, disappointed. "Couldn't you make some (excuce, excuse)? What if you (promiced, promised) to be more careful next time?"

"It's not worth the (chance, chanse)," the deckhand said. "They could (cancel, cansel) my fishing (license, licence). And besides, this guy is pretty dinky. You'd only get a few (ounces, ounses) of meat off it."

"Okay," Casey sighed. "We'll let this one go— but let's keep fishing. I have my heart set on lobster chowder for dinner!"

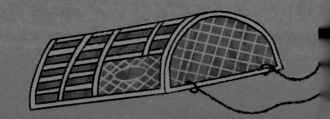

Soft c

In English, the letter *c* sometimes has an "s" sound. This is known as a soft *c*. Good spellers know when to use the soft *c* and when to use *s*.

The following word search puzzle contains the correctly spelled *c* and *s* words from the story. Find all fourteen words. Remember, if you can't find a word, you might be spelling it incorrectly.

```
U G E P Q C L O S E
X N U R N E P E C S
E C E O G O C C H U
C A Q M L X A I A C
A S W I I A N W N X
F E C S H C C T C E
R E O E S A E L E R
U A K D J T L P B E
S E S N E C I L S G
Z R Z G S E C N U O
```

Search for the correct spelling of each word:

1. surface, surfase
2. nice, nise
3. specimen, spesimen
4. releace, release
5. cace, case
6. cloce, close
7. twice, twise
8. police, polise
9. excuce, excuse
10. promiced, promised
11. chance, chanse
12. cancel, cansel
13. license, licence
14. ounces, ounses

* **Did You Know?** *
The state of Maine has laws that protect its lobster population. Size and trap limits, catch methods, and license numbers are carefully regulated.

Spelling Words

lobster	LAHB-stuhr	*noun*	a crustacean with large pincers on its first pair of legs
deckhand	DEK-hand	*noun*	a worker on a ship
shellfish	SHEL-fish	*noun*	a water animal with a hard shell
marine	muh-REEN	*adjective*	of, found in, or relating to the sea
chowder	CHAU-der	*noun*	a seafood soup with either a milk or tomato base

Snow Queen

"I don't know if I can do this," Elena said to her friend Alexis. She stared nervously past the tips of her skis at the snow-covered **slope** stretching before her.

"Sure you can!" Alexis replied. "Alpine skiing is easy, once you get the hang of it, and Dollar Mountain here is the best local place to learn. It's not as scenic as some other parts of the Sun Valley **resort**, but it's great for beginners."

"Well, that's me," sighed Elena. "I can't believe you talked me into coming on this trip."

"Come on. We'll go down the slalom course," said Alexis. "Watch me zigzag, and do what I do."

Alexis pushed off and skied slowly around a series of bars sticking out of the ground, with Elena tagging along behind. When the girls reached the end of the course, Alexis gave her friend a high five.

"You're a natural!" she exclaimed. "You'll be ready for Bald Mountain before you know it. That's where all the **intermediate** and **expert** slopes are."

"Nope, nope, nope," Elena said with a grin. "That's too adventurous for me right now. I'm happy on this bunny slope right here."

"Well then, you'd better hop to it," Alexis laughed. "Practice till you're exhausted, then practice some more. Snow bunny today . . . snow queen of Idaho tomorrow!"

Spelling Words

slope	slohp	*noun*	a slanted surface
resort	ri-ZOHRT	*noun*	a place people stay at for a vacation
intermediate	in-ter-MEE-dee-it	*adjective*	in the middle of a series or a skill range
expert	EK-spurt	*adjective*	very skilled due to experience or practice

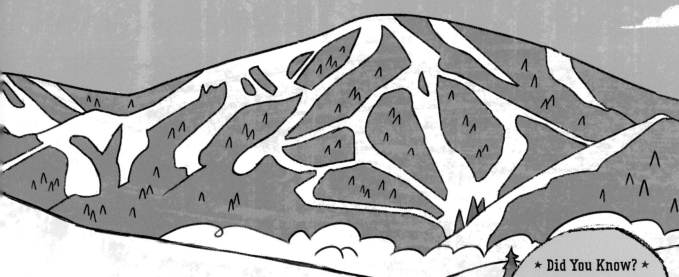

> **★ Did You Know? ★**
> Built in the 1930s, Sun Valley was one of America's first destination resorts. It boasted the nation's very first ski chairlifts.

Parts of Speech: Adjectives

Knowing a word's part of speech and definition can help you spell the word. An *adjective* is a word that describes a noun or a pronoun.

The story you just read contains six adjectives from the *Spell Across America* Index of Spelling Words (pages 84–86). Match each adjective with its definition.

1. **alpine** a. not afraid to do new things

2. **local** b. related to competitive skiing, including slalom and downhill racing

3. **scenic** c. a winding ski race with a course marked by flags

4. **slalom** d. having a nice view of nature

5. **adventurous** e. very tired

6. **exhausted** f. relating to a particular place

Answers: 1. b, 2. f, 3. d, 4. c, 5. a, 6. e

Leaf Peeping

Darnisha and her family were on a busy but scenic highway, heading to Vermont one glorious autumn weekend. They were going to visit the Green Mountains and look at the beautiful fall foliage.

"Why do leaves turn different shades?" Darnisha wondered out loud as she gazed out of the car window, looking at the kaleidoscope of colors blanketing the hills.

"When fall begins, a LEAF is green. But as the weather turns cold, the green starts to LEAK out of the leaf," her mother explained. "The leaf turns a different color, like brown, red, orange, or yellow."

"It looks like the green leaked out of *all* of them," Darnisha observed. "The trees are so bright and pretty!"

"Yes! The colors are gorgeous now. This weekend is the PEAK, or the high point, of the leaf-viewing season," her mother replied.

"That's why so many people are on their way to Vermont to take a PEEK," said Darnisha.

"That's right! Or, as they say up here, a PEEP. New Englanders call it 'leaf peeping,'" her mother said.

"Well, I sure wish this traffic would clear up so we could get there faster," Darnisha replied. "I'm ready to PEEP a LEAF or two up close."

Word Ladders, #3

Darnisha's mother made a word ladder to change the word LEAF into PEEP. Here is the word ladder:

LEAF – LEAK – PEAK – PEEK – PEEP

Can you complete these two-step word ladders?

1. **SEE** – _ _ _ – _ _ _ – **NOW**
2. **FALL** – _ _ _ _ – _ _ _ _ – **WALK**
3. **GREEN** – _ _ _ _ _ – _ _ _ _ _ – **TREAT**

Spelling Words

scenic	SEE-nik	*adjective*	having a nice view of nature
highway	HAHY-way	*noun*	a main road
mountain	MOUN-tin	*noun*	an area of land that is much higher than the area around it, and higher than a hill
foliage	FOH-lee-ij	*noun*	leaves
kaleidoscope	kuh-LAHY-duh-skohp	*noun*	a changing pattern of colors and shapes

Answers:
1. SEE – SEW – SOW – NOW
2. FALL – TALL – TALK – WALK
3. GREEN – GREET – GREAT – TREAT

Don't Trip!

Michael and his buddy José were planning an excursion to Rocky Mountain National Park in northern Colorado. The friends were determined to tackle a really big **peak** and reach its **summit**. They sat on the floor with trail maps spread around them, looking at all the options.

José pointed at one of the maps. "This **footpath** looks pretty good," he said. "But we should do more research. We have to be careful of the **route**."

"Huh? What do you mean?" said Michael. "It's the **wilderness**. There's just one?"

"Well, no, of course not," José replied. "There are lots of routes. That's why we have to be careful."

Now Michael was completely confused.

"Before, you said THE root. Just one. And why do we have to be so careful? Is it really huge or something? Do you think we might trip over it?"

José started to laugh. "I meant R-O-U-T-E, like the path we take. Not R-O-O-T, like a tree root," he said.

Michael laughed, too. "That makes more sense," he said. "You're right. We should be careful of the R-O-U-T-E and the R-O-O-T-S, too. We don't want to get hurt on our hiking adventure!"

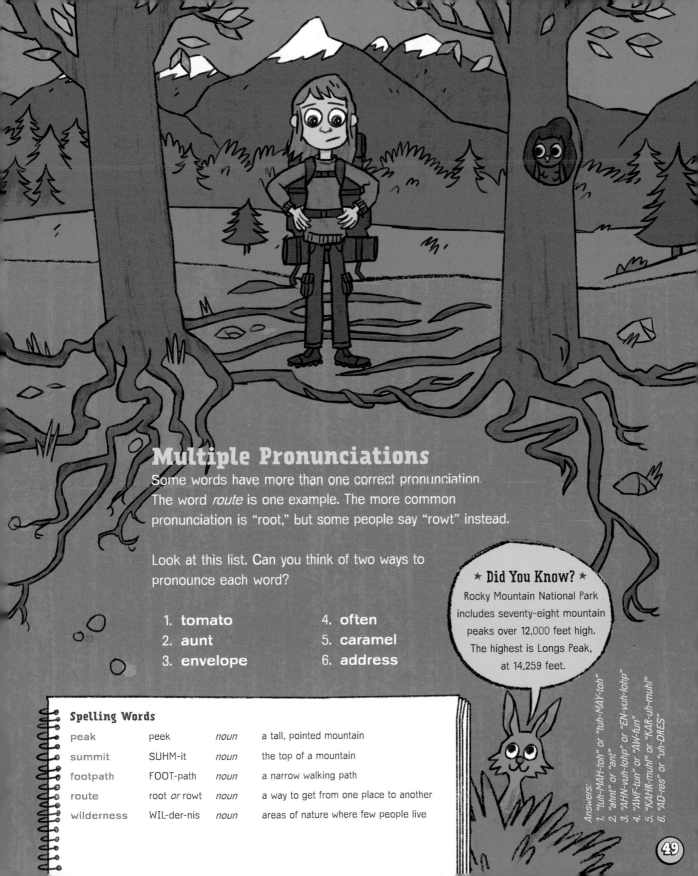

Multiple Pronunciations

Some words have more than one correct pronunciation. The word *route* is one example. The more common pronunciation is "root," but some people say "rowt" instead.

Look at this list. Can you think of two ways to pronounce each word?

1. tomato
2. aunt
3. envelope
4. often
5. caramel
6. address

Spelling Words

peak	peek	*noun*	a tall, pointed mountain
summit	SUHM-it	*noun*	the top of a mountain
footpath	FOOT-path	*noun*	a narrow walking path
route	root *or* rowt	*noun*	a way to get from one place to another
wilderness	WIL-der-nis	*noun*	areas of nature where few people live

Answers:
1. "tuh-MAH-toh" or "tuh-MAY-toh"
2. "ahnt" or "ant"
3. "AHN-vuh-lohp" or "EN-vuh-lohp"
4. "AWF-tun" or "AW-fun"
5. "KAHR-muhl" or "KAR-uh-muhl"
6. "AD-res" or "uh-DRES"

Tall Tree Tales

"Man, this is one big tree," said Lori. She craned her neck backward and squinted to focus on the leafy canopy high above.

"It sure is," said Lori's uncle. "And these big **sequoias** are ancient, too. This particular tree is **antique**, at over two thousand years old! Between their age and their size, sequoias definitely qualify as **natural** wonders. People come from all over to see them here in California's Sequoia National Park."

"I can see why," Lori replied. "The sign here says this tree is almost three hundred feet tall! That's like, what, a quarter of a mile?"

"No, three hundred feet isn't quite that tall,"

Lori's uncle laughed. "But these trees are **unique**—that's for sure. I bet it would be hard for a squirrel to conquer this climb."

Lori laughed, too. "The climb wouldn't be quick," she agreed. "It would take forever to get to the top of that thing."

"Well, luckily, we don't have to climb the tree. I don't think I'd have nearly the skill or **endurance** needed for that task," said Lori's uncle. "I'm perfectly happy enjoying it from the ground."

"Me too," said Lori with a smile. "Let's enjoy this tall tree from right where we are—no climbing required!"

qu Words: "kw" or "k"?

The letter combination *qu* makes different sounds in different words. In most words, it makes a "kw" sound: *quiet, squeeze, frequent*. In some words, it makes a "k" sound: *queue, quiche, opaque*. Occasionally, it can be pronounced both ways, depending on the speaker: *quart* is usually pronounced "kort," but sometimes "kwart."

The story you just read contains eleven words in which the *qu* combination makes a "kw" or "k" sound. Can you spot all of the *qu* words? Now say them aloud. Which do you think make the "kw" sound? What about the "k" sound? Remember that pronunciations may vary regionally—in at least two of these words, the *qu* combination can make either the "kw" or "k" sound!

"kw" sounds

1. _____   5. _____

2. _____   6. _____

3. _____   7. _____

4. _____

"k" sounds

1. _____

2. _____

3. _____

4. _____

★ **Did You Know?** ★

By volume, the General Sherman Tree in Sequoia National Park is the world's largest tree. It is 274.9 feet high and 36.5 feet in diameter at the base.

Spelling Words

sequoia	si-KWOI-uh *or* si-KOI-uh	*noun*	a very tall Californian evergreen tree
antique	an-TEEK	*adjective*	from a long time ago
natural	NA-chuhr-uhl	*adjective*	of or relating to the parts of the world and things in the world that are not made by people
unique	yoo-NEEK	*adjective*	special, unusual, or unlike anything else
endurance	en-DOO-ruhns	*noun*	the ability to do something for a long time

Answers: "kw" sounds: squirted, qualify, quite, squirrel, quick, required. "k" sounds: antique, unique, conquer, sequoia. Either "k" or "kw" sounds: sequoias. Since pronunciations may vary regionally, it's okay if some of your answers differ from ours!

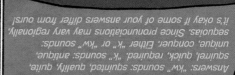

Letters on Parade

It's Super Secret Spelling Day again! Jodie has gone with her family to New Orleans, Louisiana, to watch the annual Mardi Gras parade. Jodie loves the event's proud display of the region's **bayou** and **Creole** traditions—and so do lots of other people, it seems! Huge crowds are lined up along the **avenue**. Jodie munches on a tasty **beignet** as she waits for the **jazz** music and marching to begin.

Because it is Super Secret Spelling Day, the performers in the parade can only do things that contain a certain letter sound. Can you guess what it is?

- ▶ They can drum, but not blow.
- ▶ They can dance, but not shake.
- ▶ They can step, but not stride.
- ▶ They can grin, but not smile.
- ▶ They can wink, but not wave.
- ▶ They can sing, but not pipe.
- ▶ They can walk, but not ride.
- ▶ They can clap, but not sway.
- ▶ They can jump, but not jive.
- ▶ They can sniff, but not sneeze.

Answer: The performers can do things that contain short vowel sounds. The word juggle has a short u, so Jodie should get ready for a show!

Jodie is wondering one thing: Will the performers be able to juggle? What do you think?

52

Spelling Words

bayou	BAHY-yoo	*noun*	a very slow-moving area of water in the southern United States
Creole	KREE-ohl	*adjective*	related to the culture of the descendants of early French or Spanish settlers in the U.S. Gulf
avenue	AV-uh-noo	*noun*	a wide street
beignet	bayn-YAY	*noun*	a doughnut sprinkled with powdered sugar
jazz	jaz	*noun*	a type of American music that includes parts that are made up by musicians in the moment

★ **Did You Know?** ★
In 2005, Hurricane Katrina flooded and destroyed much of New Orleans. Today, most of the damage is repaired, and the city's rich traditions continue.

Long and Short Vowel Sounds

Long vowels sound like their name: long *a* = "ay," long *e* = "ee," long *i* = "eye," long *o* = "oh," and long *u* = "you" or "oo." Short vowels sound like anything else.

Look at each word pair below. Which word has the long vowel sound? Which word has a short vowel sound?

1. band   play
2. scene   best
3. size   six

4. pot   post
5. sun   cute

Long vowel sounds: 1. play, 2. scene, 3. size, 4. post, 5. cute
Short vowel sounds: 1. band, 2. best, 3. six, 4. pot, 5. sun

53

A Lasting Impression

"They're amazing—that's for sure," said Phil as he looked at the four stone faces carved into the South Dakota hillside. "But what's the point of it?"

"According to the **brochure**, the purpose of the Mount Rushmore National **Memorial** is 'to communicate the founding, expansion, preservation, and unification of the United States,'" read Phil's father.

"Phew! That's a lot of big words," said Phil.

"Well, I guess that makes sense. Mount Rushmore was a big vision," his father replied. "From **conception** to completion, the construction took fourteen years."

"How did they make such a huge **sculpture**?" Phil asked.

"Workers used **dynamite** to remove big chunks of rock," his father said. "Then they used smaller tools to complete each impression."

"That was a smart solution," Phil said. "It obviously worked, because here are all these presidents—Washington, Jefferson, Roosevelt, and Lincoln—on display for everyone to see."

"Yes. And Mount Rushmore has become a big attraction," Phil's father said. "Over two million people visit each year."

"Including us," said Phil. "I'm glad we're here. In my wildest imagination, I never dreamed a big rock could be so cool!"

★ Did You Know? ★
The faces of Mount Rushmore are 60 feet high. That's the height of a six-story building!

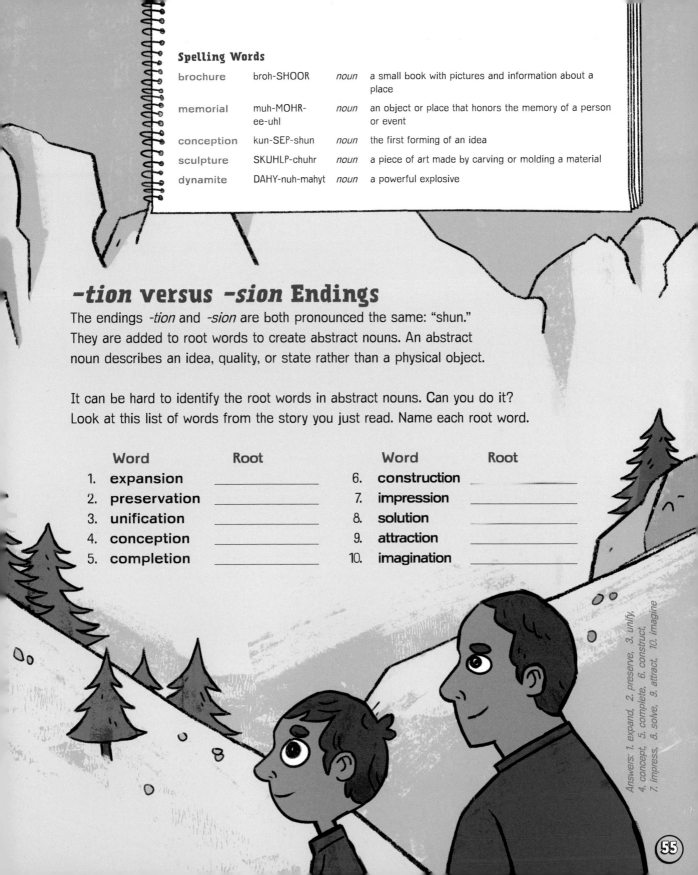

Spelling Words

brochure	broh-SHOOR	*noun*	a small book with pictures and information about a place
memorial	muh-MOHR-ee-uhl	*noun*	an object or place that honors the memory of a person or event
conception	kun-SEP-shun	*noun*	the first forming of an idea
sculpture	SKUHLP-chuhr	*noun*	a piece of art made by carving or molding a material
dynamite	DAHY-nuh-mahyt	*noun*	a powerful explosive

-tion versus -sion Endings

The endings *-tion* and *-sion* are both pronounced the same: "shun."
They are added to root words to create abstract nouns. An abstract
noun describes an idea, quality, or state rather than a physical object.

It can be hard to identify the root words in abstract nouns. Can you do it?
Look at this list of words from the story you just read. Name each root word.

	Word	Root		Word	Root
1.	expansion	_____	6.	construction	_____
2.	preservation	_____	7.	impression	_____
3.	unification	_____	8.	solution	_____
4.	conception	_____	9.	attraction	_____
5.	completion	_____	10.	imagination	_____

Answers: 1. expand, 2. preserve, 3. unify, 4. concept, 5. complete, 6. construct, 7. impress, 8. solve, 9. attract, 10. imagine

Flying Fish

"Hoy!" grunted a worker as he hurled a massive salmon across the **seafood** stand. The watching crowd gasped in delight as the fish landed—*plunk!*—on a table to be wrapped and sold.

"Wow!" said Iris. "I'm impressed!"

"You and about ten million other people every year," Iris's aunt replied with a smile. "The Pike Place **Market** is Seattle's most popular **attraction**, and the flying fish are world famous."

"All those people come to see guys throwing fish?" Iris asked, skeptical.

"Well, it's not just that," her aunt said. "Besides this fish stand, there are about five hundred shops in the **bazaar**. You can buy practically anything here—fresh produce, crafts,

bath products, books, you name it. And the stalls are all family businesses, which makes this place really special."

"Our family should open one," Iris said. "That would be fun!"

"We could," her aunt answered. "Or you could just come work in *this* **stall** and learn to toss fish."

"No, thanks! They're too slimy for me," Iris laughed. "On the other hand, *eating* one of those fish—I could handle that. Let's go to that seafood restaurant I saw out front. I'm ready for a fish to fly right off my plate . . . and into my mouth!"

Word Origins, #4

Knowing a word's origin can help you understand how to spell it. The word *bazaar* comes from the Persian word *bazar*, which means "market." It refers to an outdoor shopping area with rows of small booths that sell many different kinds of goods.

Read these definitions of English words that originated in Arab countries. Can you figure out the word that matches each definition?

1. A group of vehicles traveling together   c _ _ _ v _ n
2. A magical being that lives in a bottle   g _ n _ _
3. A type of math   a _ _ _ b r _
4. A trip into the wilderness to see animals   s _ _ a r _
5. A popular morning drink   c _ _ f _ _

> ★ **Did You Know?** ★
> Pike Place Market sprawls across nine acres. It includes eleven buildings and six levels.

Spelling Words

seafood	SEE-food	*noun*	animals that live in the ocean and are used for food
market	MAHR-kit	*noun*	a place to buy things
attraction	uh-TRAK-shuhn	*noun*	something fun to visit, see, or do
bazaar	buh-ZAHR	*noun*	a market with lots of shops selling different things
stall	stahl	*noun*	a booth or stand

Answers: 1. caravan, 2. genie, 3. algebra, 4. safari, 5. coffee

Over the Bridge

Niall and his buddy Keith had already walked a mile—but there was still a long way to go.

"How long is this bridge, anyway?" Niall grumbled.

"The Golden Gate **Bridge** is (large, lardge)—that's for sure," Keith answered. "It's almost two miles long! Building this thing was quite a **construction** feat. The bridge opened in 1937 to help people get from San Francisco to Marin County. Before the bridge, they had to take a **ferry**."

"And now they can just (truge, trudge) across, like us," Niall said.

"Yep. Or bike, or drive, or take a bus," Keith said. "The bridge gets all kinds of (usage, usadge). There's a (charge, chardge) to drive across, but walking is free."

"Why are the **cables** (orange, orandge)?" Niall said.

"It's not just for looks—although the color *has* helped to make this bridge a popular (image, imadge)," Keith replied. "The bright color makes the cables easy to see in the **fog**, so it's a safety feature. Workers touch up the paint all the time to keep it fresh."

"Wow," said Niall, gazing at the pillars towering above the bridge's deck. "Can you (imagine, imadgine) getting stuck with that job?"

"No way," Keith answered. "I'm not (buging, budging) from this nice, flat sidewalk."

"Me neither," Niall agreed. "I don't mind being near the (ege, edge), but I don't need to be up above it. The view from right here is incredible—and so is this bridge. I'm glad we took the (plunge, plundge) and decided to take this walk!"

g versus dg

In English, the letter *g* sometimes has a "j" sound. This is known as a soft *g*. The letter combination *dg* can also have a "j" sound. Do you know which spelling to use? Let's find out!

The following word search puzzle contains the correctly spelled *g* and *dg* words from the story. Find all eleven words. Remember, if you can't find a word, you might be spelling it incorrectly.

P	S	X	B	R	I	D	G	E	C
E	E	R	N	G	A	P	I	U	H
U	E	G	N	A	R	O	M	T	A
E	S	S	A	P	M	F	A	D	R
D	G	A	T	M	F	V	G	E	G
G	L	D	G	E	I	S	I	G	E
E	A	C	U	E	G	M	N	D	X
Z	R	C	Q	R	M	D	E	U	I
M	G	E	G	B	T	D	A	B	C
V	E	G	N	U	L	P	D	G	F

Search for the correct spelling of each word:

1. large, lardge
2. truge, trudge
3. usage, usadge
4. charge, chardge
5. orange, orandge
6. image, imadge
7. imagine, imadgine
8. buging, budging
9. ege, edge
10. plunge, plundge

Spelling Words

bridge	brij	*noun*	a road that goes over a body of water or other obstacle
construction	kuhn-STRUHK-shuhn	*noun*	the process of building
ferry	FAYR-ee	*noun*	a boat that carries people or things between two places
cable	KAY-bl	*noun*	a strong wire rope
fog	fahg	*noun*	a mass of small water drops floating in the air

Get in Line

"What? Ninety minutes? Can that possibly be right?" Naomi wailed.

"That's what the sign says," her mother replied. "I'm afraid that's how long we'll wait in line for this **roller coaster**."

"That's forever," Naomi grumbled. "These Orlando **theme** parks are cool, but they're really crowded."

Her mother laughed. "They sure are. It's because they are super popular. People come from all over the world to visit these attractions," she said.

"Well, ninety minutes is too long. Let's find another way to amuse ourselves," Naomi said.

"I'm sure we won't have any trouble with that." Naomi's mother smiled. "There are all kinds of things to ride here. Some of them carry a lot more **passengers** than this coaster, so the lines should be way shorter."

"Okay. Let's go!" Naomi replied. "We'll do all the rides with short lines first—and then, if there's time, we can come back to the roller coaster. I want to pack as much fun as possible into our Florida vacation!"

Parts of Speech: Verbs

Knowing a word's part of speech and definition can help you spell the word.
A *verb* is a word that describes an action.

The story you just read contains six verbs from the *Spell Across America*
Index of Spelling Words (pages 84–86). Match each verb with its definition.

1. **wait**   a. to go somewhere or see someone

2. **visit**   b. to fill completely

3. **amuse**   c. to travel as a passenger in or on something

4. **ride**   d. to stay until it is your turn to do something

5. **carry**   e. to entertain

6. **pack**   f. to move something while holding it

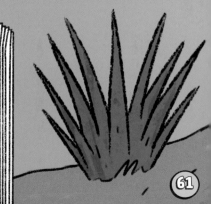

> ★ **Did You Know?** ★
> Orlando is one of the world's
> top tourist attractions, and it
> seems to grow in popularity
> every year. In 1995, the city
> received about 32 million
> visitors. By 2015, that number
> had more than doubled, to
> over 66 million!

Spelling Words

roller coaster	ROH-ler koh-ster	*noun*	an amusement park ride with a train moving along a high, curving track
theme	theem	*adjective*	the main subject or idea of something
passenger	PAS-in-juhr	*noun*	a person traveling in (but not driving) a vehicle

WELCOME TO
Luray
Caverns

Safe and Sound

Trace stared into the cave's black mouth. He had been longing to visit Luray Caverns in Virginia for years. Now he was here, about to do a little **spelunking**. He was excited—but scared, too.

"Are you sure we won't get lost?" Trace asked the **guide** he had hired to lead him into the cave's dark depths.

"I'm positive," said the guide. "For one thing, we have **lanterns**. Also, I've been in this cave a hundred times—I think I know the location of every single **stalactite** and **stalagmite**! But even if I weren't so familiar with this particular cavern, it's easy to keep from getting lost in a cave."

"How?" asked Trace.

"The best way to avoid getting LOST is to buy the best ropes, no matter the COST," the guide said.

"Okay," said Trace. "And then what?"

"You tie those ropes to the cave entrance. You CAST them behind you as you explore. They mark your trail in CASE you get confused. If that happens, you just follow the ropes back out of the CAVE. Problem solved!"

"That makes sense," said Trace. "I can certainly see why you would use the best ropes. No one wants to get LOST in a CAVE. Which we won't, for sure—at least not today. Let's explore!"

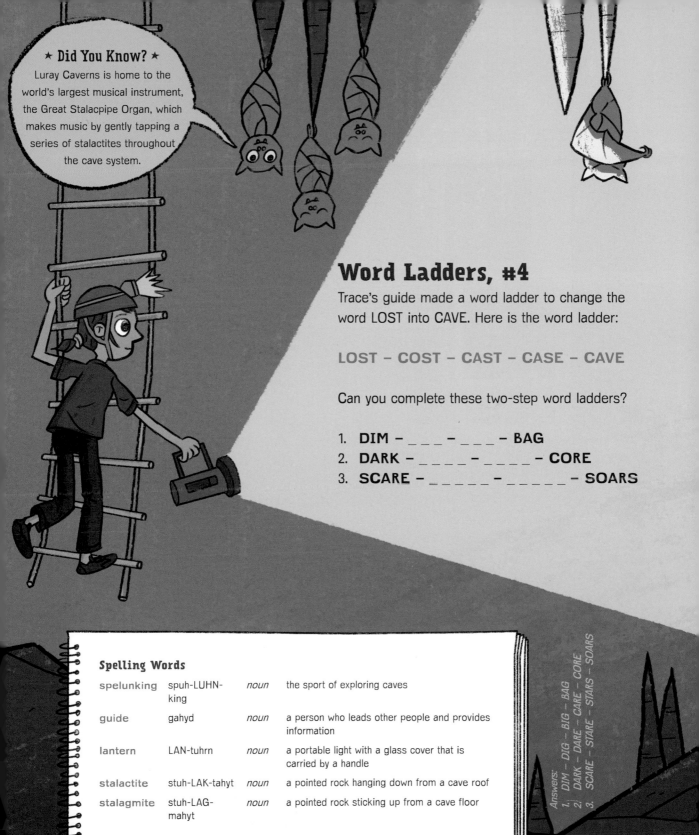

Word Ladders, #4

Trace's guide made a word ladder to change the word LOST into CAVE. Here is the word ladder:

LOST – COST – CAST – CASE – CAVE

Can you complete these two-step word ladders?

1. **DIM** – _ _ _ – _ _ _ – **BAG**
2. **DARK** – _ _ _ _ – _ _ _ _ – **CORE**
3. **SCARE** – _ _ _ _ _ – _ _ _ _ _ – **SOARS**

Spelling Words

spelunking	spuh-LUHN-king	*noun*	the sport of exploring caves
guide	gahyd	*noun*	a person who leads other people and provides information
lantern	LAN-tuhrn	*noun*	a portable light with a glass cover that is carried by a handle
stalactite	stuh-LAK-tahyt	*noun*	a pointed rock hanging down from a cave roof
stalagmite	stuh-LAG-mahyt	*noun*	a pointed rock sticking up from a cave floor

Answers:
1. DIM – DIG – BIG – BAG
2. DARK – DARE – CARE – CORE
3. SCARE – STARE – STARS – SOARS

A Nice Place to Stay

The summer was coming to an end, and Amanda's big brother, Sean, had just returned from the adventure of a lifetime. Sean was a biology major, and he had gone on a college study trip to Hawaii. He had spent a month on the island of Maui.

"The tropical **flora** and **fauna** are amazing," Sean told his sister. "Pineapples and sugarcane grew wild all over the place. And these funny Hawaiian geese called nenes were walking around. It was cool."

"It sounds like heaven," Amanda said. "But a whole month—wasn't that really expensive?"

"It wasn't too bad. We stayed at a **hostel** instead of a hotel to save money," Sean replied.

"That doesn't sound very nice," Amanda said, frowning.

"They definitely didn't offer every **amenity**," Sean admitted. "But the people were so friendly."

"That makes no sense," Amanda said, confused. "If everyone was so friendly, why was it called a **hostile**? It sounds so mean!"

Sean grinned. "I get what you're saying! Not an H-O-S-T-I-L-E, funny girl. An H-O-S-T-E-L. It's like a dormitory for travelers. Everyone shares the bathrooms and bedrooms, so it's super cheap to stay there."

"Oh! I've never heard of those before," Amanda said.

"They're all over the place. I'll take you to one when you're old enough," Sean laughed. "You'll see that the guests aren't HOSTILE at all—I promise!"

★ **Did You Know?** ★
The length of the Hawaiian Archipelago is 1,523 miles. It includes eight main islands and over a hundred smaller islets.

Hard versus Soft *i*

In most words ending with the letters -*le*, the vowel before the -*le* combination has a long sound—it is pronounced "I'll," like the contraction for "I will." In American English, the word *hostile* is one of several exceptions. The letter *i* in this word usually has a short sound—it is most often pronounced "ill," like the synonym for *sick*.

Look at the -*ile* words on this list. Read each one out loud. Which ones can end in the soft "ill" sound? Which ones end in a hard "I'll" sound?

1. **profile**
2. **reptile**
3. **fertile**
4. **smile**
5. **missile**
6. **agile**
7. **exile**
8. **fragile**

★ **Fun Fact** ★
Pronunciation is different in British English. All of the "ill" words on this list are pronounced with an "I'll" sound on "the other side of the pond." How confusing!

Answers: (Remember that there can be some variation here.)
Soft i: fertile, missile, fragile, agile
Hard i: profile, reptile, smile, exile

Spelling Words

flora	FLOH-ruh	*noun*	all the plants that live in a certain place
fauna	FAH-nuh	*noun*	all the animals that live in a certain place
hostel	HAHS-til	*noun*	an inexpensive place to stay overnight
amenity	uh-MEN-uh-tee	*noun*	a feature that provides comfort or convenience
hostile	HAHS-til	*adjective*	unfriendly

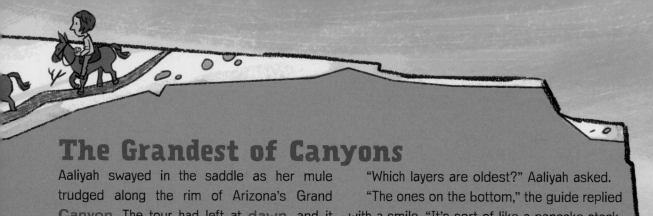

The Grandest of Canyons

Aaliyah swayed in the saddle as her mule trudged along the rim of Arizona's Grand **Canyon**. The tour had left at **dawn**, and it was moving slowly—but Aaliyah didn't mind. There was a long, long drop to her left. She was happy that the **mules** were being so careful.

"Let's stop here, everyone," called the guide from the front of the line. "I want to show you some interesting **geology**."

The guide pointed at the canyon's wall. "See how the rocks are arranged in layers? There are red stripes and yellow ones and brown ones. Each layer formed during a different period of our planet's history."

"Which layers are oldest?" Aaliyah asked.

"The ones on the bottom," the guide replied with a smile. "It's sort of like a pancake stack. The lowest layers are hundreds of millions of years old. Some of them contain **fossils**."

"That's neat!" Aaliyah said. "Can we see some?"

"Yes," said the guide. "There are some great fossils just beyond this next bend. And there's a shady place to rest, too. The Grand Canyon has been here for eons—it can wait another few minutes while we cool off!"

The Letter *y*: Consonant or Vowel?

The letter *y* is the only letter in the English language that can function as either a vowel or a consonant. It follows these rules:

▶ If the *y* has an "ee" sound, it's usually a vowel.
▶ If the *y* has a "yuh" sound, it's usually a consonant.
▶ If a word ends with a vowel-*y* combination, like E-Y or O-Y, the *y* is a consonant.
▶ If the *y* provides the only vowel sound in a syllable, it's a vowel.

The story you just read includes nine words where *y* functions as a consonant, and six words where *y* functions as a vowel. Can you spot all of them?

y as a consonant
1. _____
2. _____
3. _____
4. _____
5. _____
6. _____
7. _____
8. _____
9. _____

y as a vowel
1. _____
2. _____
3. _____
4. _____
5. _____
6. _____

Answers: y as a consonant: Aaliyah, swayed, canyon, you, layers, yellow, years, yes, beyond
y as a vowel: slowly, happy, everyone, geology, history, shady

Spelling Words

canyon	KAN-yuhn	*noun*	a deep valley made of rock
dawn	dahn	*noun*	the time when the sun begins to come up
mule	myool	*noun*	a cross between a horse and a donkey
geology	jee-AH-luh-jee	*noun*	a science that studies rocks and soil
fossil	FAH-sil	*noun*	something from an ancient plant or animal that you can see in rocks

Snoozing Zoo

It is Super Secret Spelling Day again, and Kae and her family are going to visit the world-famous San Diego Zoo in California. Kae is looking forward to seeing animals from the **rain forest** and the **Arctic** and everything in between. It'll be like a one-day **safari**! But there's just one small problem: Only animals whose names contain a certain type of letter are awake today. Look at this list of animals that are and are not awake. Can you figure out the secret?

- ▶ The lambs are awake, but not the sheep.
- ▶ The wrens are awake, but not the parrots.
- ▶ The **gnus** are awake, but not the deer.
- ▶ The leopards are awake, but not the lions.
- ▶ The tortoises are awake, but not the warthogs.
- ▶ The rhinos are awake, but not the hippos.
- ▶ The cheetahs are awake, but not the bears.
- ▶ The pheasants are awake, but not the anteaters.
- ▶ The salmon are awake, but not the tuna.
- ▶ The **chameleons** are awake, but not the frogs.

So Kae wonders just one thing: Will she get to feed the birds in the aviary a treat? Why or why not? Can you name the secret spelling rule?

Answer: The names of the awake animals contain silent letters. The word birds has no silent letters, so the birds are all fast asleep today. No treats for them!

★ **Did You Know?** ★
The San Diego Zoo houses more than 3,700 rare and endangered animals, representing 650 species and subspecies.

Spelling Words

rain forest	RAYN fohr-ist	*noun*	a tropical forest with very tall trees and lots of rain
Arctic	AHRK-tik	*noun*	the region around the North Pole
safari	suh-FAHR-ee	*noun*	a journey to explore and observe nature in eastern Africa
gnu	noo	*noun*	a large African animal with curved horns; a wildebeest
chameleon	kuh-MEE-lee-un	*noun*	a lizard with the ability to change the color of its skin

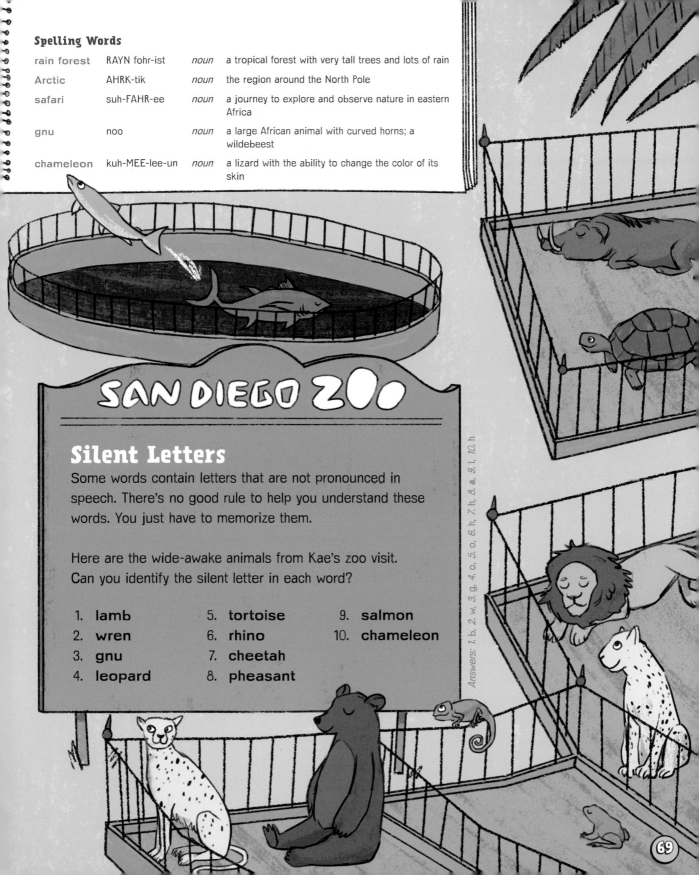

SAN DIEGO ZOO

Silent Letters

Some words contain letters that are not pronounced in speech. There's no good rule to help you understand these words. You just have to memorize them.

Here are the wide-awake animals from Kae's zoo visit. Can you identify the silent letter in each word?

1. lamb
2. wren
3. gnu
4. leopard
5. tortoise
6. rhino
7. cheetah
8. pheasant
9. salmon
10. chameleon

69

An Unreal View

"Look at me! There are four of me!" Willem exclaimed. He jumped up and down on the round slab that marked the **intersection** of Arizona, Colorado, Utah, and New Mexico—the only place in America where four states touch.

"Untrue," laughed Willem's sister, Trina. "You may be standing in four states, but you're not four people. That's impossible."

"Ah, but I am abnormally talented," Willem responded. "I defy all natural laws." He jumped some more and waved his arms grandly at the vast open **plateau** surrounding the Four Corners Monument.

"It almost looks like this scenery is disregarding the laws of nature, too," sighed Trina. "These colors are unbelievable."

"They really are," said Trina's mother, who had just emerged from the family's recreational **vehicle**. "The sun reflects off the desert **sandstone** to create all kinds of shades. The view here is incomparable. But it's not too shabby from the nearby **campgrounds**, either."

"Is that a hint?" Trina said with a smile.

"Maybe," her mother replied, smiling back. "I'm ready to relax."

"I'm unsurprised," Trina said. "It's been a long day. The only question is, which state should we sleep in? It looks like we have four great choices!"

Negative Prefixes

Certain prefixes, when added to a word, create a new word with the opposite meaning. The story you just read contains many words with negative prefixes.

This list includes some prefixes that were used in the story and some that were not. Can you name one word that starts with each negative prefix?

1. ab_____
2. anti_____
3. dis_____
4. dys_____
5. im_____

6. mal_____
7. mis_____
8. non_____
9. un_____
10. sub_____

Spelling Words

intersection	IN-tuhr-sek-shuhn	*noun*	a place where two or more things cross
plateau	pla-TOH	*noun*	a large, high, flat area of land
vehicle	VEE-hi-kuhl	*noun*	a machine that carries people or things from one place to another
sandstone	SAND-stohn	*noun*	a soft stone made of sand
campground	KAMP-ground	*noun*	an outdoor area where people can put up tents or park campers

Examples: 1. abnormal. 2. antibacterial. 3. disagree. 4. dystopian. 5. impossible. 6. maladjusted. 7. misalign. 8. nonexistent. 9. unwanted. 10. substandard

Just Chilling Out

Alex stood on the cruise ship's **deck**, shivering in the wind's icy blast.

"I can't believe it's this cold in July," he muttered.

"Hey, it's never all that warm in Alaska," Alex's dad replied. "And it's especially cold when you're right in front of a **glacier**. Hubbard Glacier is a huge column of ice more than seventy miles long. The Arctic wind blows across all that ice—and then down onto us. It's like a natural air conditioner."

"I wish we could get a closer look," Alex said, staring at the blue-tinged wall of ice on the opposite side of the bay. "Why do we have to stay so far away?"

Just then, a loud *crack!* **echoed** across the water. A huge chunk of ice broke away from the glacier and tumbled into the sea.

"That's why! A new **iceberg** is born," said Alex's dad. "It doesn't look so big from here, but the glacier's wall is forty stories high! That iceberg is probably the size of a building."

"Okay, I get it." Alex grinned. "I've read about the *Titanic*. I know that ships and icebergs aren't a good combination."

"Nope," laughed Alex's dad. "Ships make great glacier viewing spots, but only from a safe distance. I'm happy chilling out right here—literally. I sure am glad I brought my jacket!"

Word Origins, #5

Knowing a word's origin can help you understand how to spell it. The word *glacier* comes from the Old French word *glace*, which means "ice."

Read these definitions of English words and terms with French origins. Can you figure out the word or term that matches each definition?

1. A paid, professional driver **c _ _ _ f f _ _ r**
2. An actor's first performance **d _ _ _ t**
3. A main meal at a restaurant **e _ t _ é e**
4. A meet-up between two people **r _ _ d _ z v _ _ s**
5. A dead end **c _ l -_ _ -s _ _**

Cruise Alaska

Spelling Words

deck	dek	*noun*	the flat outside floor on a boat or ship
glacier	GLAY-shuhr	*noun*	a large area of ice slowly moving down a slope
echo	EH-koh	*verb*	to repeat sounds
iceberg	AHYS-burg	*noun*	a very large piece of ice in the ocean

Answers: 1. chauffeur, 2. debut,
3. entrée, 4. rendezvous,
5. cul-de-sac

Ooh! Aah!

"Why is she green and (bloo, blue, blew)?" asked Cole, gazing at the sculpture towering above him. "Is that (mildoo, mildue, mildew)?"

Cole's uncle smiled at his nephew. "It looks like she could use a good (shampoo, shampue, shampew), doesn't it?" he said. "But the green stuff isn't something that (groo, grue, grew) on the Statue of Liberty. She's made of **copper**. The colorful coating is called **verdigris**, and it's sort of like rust."

"Will (yoo, you, yew) hand me the binoculars, please? I want to take a closer look," Cole said.

Cole lifted the **binoculars** to his eyes and peered at the statue while his uncle kept talking.

"At first, people thought the green was a sign of damage. A work (croo, crue, crew) was hired to (renoo, renou, renew) the statue. But then officials realized the verdigris was helpful, not harmful. It actually protected the copper. So they decided not to (pursoo, pursue, pursew) the renovation."

"Are you making that up?" Cole asked, skeptical.

"Every word is (troo, true, trew)," Cole's uncle laughed. "Ol' green Lady Liberty here has become a symbol of our culture. She stands in New York **Harbor** to welcome **immigrants** to America."

"That's a nice sight for (noo, nou, new) arrivals—and for me, (tew, too, tou)," said Cole. "Copper, green, or any other color, this big statue is definitely worth seeing with my own (tew, tou, two) eyes!"

★ **Did You Know?** ★
The Statue of Liberty was a gift of friendship from France to the United States. It was dedicated on October 28, 1886.

"oo" Sounds

The "oo" sound is spelled many ways in English. It can be spelled with a double *o*: *taboo, yahoo*. Other common spellings include *ue* (*subdue, glue*) and *ew* (*flew, drew*). Can you tell them apart?

The following word search puzzle contains the correctly spelled "oo" words from the story. Find all twelve words. Remember, if you can't find a word, you might be spelling it incorrectly.

W	Z	E	Q	U	J	D	S	W	P
E	C	U	G	R	E	W	U	U	E
N	S	S	C	Z	E	U	R	T	G
E	H	R	W	D	O	W	T	P	R
R	A	U	P	C	R	E	W	H	I
J	M	P	Y	O	U	D	N	D	N
V	P	N	G	L	T	L	X	X	Z
I	O	K	B	R	Q	I	R	N	V
A	O	C	K	W	Z	M	E	Z	N
T	O	O	X	Y	Z	W	Y	I	C

Search for the correct spelling of each word:

1. bloo, blue, blew
2. mildoo, mildue, mildew
3. shampoo, shampue, shampew
4. groo, grue, grew
5. you, yoo, yew
6. croo, crue, crew
7. renoo, renou, renew
8. pursoo, pursue, pursew
9. troo, true, trew
10. noo, nou, new
11. tew, too, tou
12. tew, tou, two

Spelling Words

copper	KAHP-er	*noun*	a common reddish-brown metallic element
verdigris	VUR-duh-gree	*noun*	a green or greenish-blue pigment formed on copper
binoculars	bahy-NAHK-yuh-luhrz	*plural noun*	a device made of two telescopes that helps you see far away
harbor	HAHR-buhr	*noun*	part of a body of water next to land that is deep enough for ships
immigrant	IM-uh-grunt	*noun*	a person who comes to a country to live there

Tough Tour

"Ow, ow, ow! My legs are killing me," Todd complained as he got ready to **pump** up his **bicycle**'s tires in front of the North Carolina inn where he and his big sister, Sarah, had spent the night with their family.

"I'm not surprised," laughed Sarah. "We biked a lot of miles yesterday, and the Great Smoky Mountains are hilly! This Blue Ridge Parkway tour is a tough **endeavor**, that's for sure. But I hoped your legs would feel better overnight."

"Maybe a little bit," Todd admitted. "But they still hurt."

"Well, hang in there for one more day! We're heading homeward now," Sarah replied. "And we don't have to push ourselves. We can just take it slowly and safely."

"Oh, I can go fast—as long as we're riding downhill," Todd said with a grin.

"There will be plenty of downhill stretches," Sarah said. "But we'll have to ride uphill, too. We're in the mountains, after all."

"I know," Todd sighed. "I hope my legs will feel better after I **stretch** and warm up. And I *know* they'll feel better tonight, when we get home. This tour has been amazing—but I'm ready to get off this bicycle seat and into my **comfortable** bed!"

Parts of Speech: Adverbs

Knowing a word's part of speech and definition can help you spell the word. An *adverb* is a word that modifies a verb, an adjective, or another adverb. It usually answers questions like "How?" "Where?" "When?" or "How much?"

The story you just read contains six adverbs from the *Spell Across America* Index of Spelling Words (pages 84–86). Match each adverb with its definition.

1. **overnight**
2. **homeward**
3. **slowly**
4. **safely**
5. **downhill**
6. **uphill**

a. in a manner without danger
b. toward the top of a hill
c. toward home
d. toward the bottom of a hill
e. at a low speed
f. for the entire night

Answers: 1. f, 2. c, 3. e, 4. a, 5. d, 6. b

Spelling Words

pump	pump	*verb*	to inflate using an up-and-down or back-and-forth motion
bicycle	BAHY-si-kuhl	*noun*	a human-powered vehicle with two wheels and foot pedals
endeavor	en-DEV-er	*noun*	an attempt with much effort
stretch	strech	*verb*	to extend or reach out
comfortable	KUM-fer-tuh-bl	*adjective*	relaxed and free from unpleasant feelings

Start Your Engines

Only one minute to go! Josef had always dreamed of seeing an **automobile** race at the Indianapolis Motor Speedway. He and his father had **traveled** all the way across Indiana to attend today's event . . . and the big moment was almost here!

Josef's father had never been to a **speedway** before, and he wasn't much of a race fan, but he was trying to learn.

"Explain to me again why these car drivers are famous?" he asked his son.

"Well, in this RACE, they drive at a super-fast RATE. They have to **accelerate** hard, right out of the GATE," Josef explained.

"But what's so hard about that? After the cars get started, they just steer in big circles," Josef's dad replied.

"It might seem like that. But car racing is like a GAME. There's lots of strategy involved," Josef said. "And everyone knows the best player's NAME, and that leads to FAME."

At that moment, a voice blared over the **loudspeaker**.

"Drivers, start your engines!" it cried. Dozens of car engines immediately roared to life.

"Just watch and see," Josef shouted over the din.

"I will," Josef's father shouted back. "I'm ready to have a famously good time with my son!"

Spelling Words

automobile	AH-tuh-moh-beel	*noun*	a car
travel	TRA-vuhl	*verb*	to go on a trip
speedway	SPEED-way	*noun*	a track where vehicles race
accelerate	ak-SEL-uh-rayt	*verb*	to speed up
loudspeaker	LAUD-speek-er	*noun*	a device that projects sound to people in a public space

★ **Did You Know?** ★
The Indianapolis Motor Speedway was originally paved with bricks. Today a three-foot-wide strip of the original bricks remains to mark the start/finish line.

Word Ladders, #5

Josef made a word ladder to change the word RACE into FAME. Here is the word ladder:

RACE – RATE – GATE – GAME – NAME – FAME

Can you complete these tricky three-step word ladders?

1. **CREW** – _ _ _ _ – _ _ _ _ – _ _ _ _ – **SHOP**
2. **CARS** – _ _ _ _ – _ _ _ _ – _ _ _ _ – **RAMP**
3. **FAST** – _ _ _ _ – _ _ _ _ – _ _ _ _ – **NOSE**

Answers:
1. CREW – CHEW – CHOW – CHOP – SHOP
2. CARS – JARS – JAMS – RAMS – RAMP
3. FAST – LAST – LOST – LOSE – NOSE

A Capital Time

"What are we doing today?" Omar asked his grandfather. The pair had been on **vacation** in Washington, D.C., for two days already. They had seen lots of things, but there was so much more to do! Omar couldn't wait to hear which **monument** or **landmark** they might visit next.

"I thought we could tour the **Capitol**," Omar's grandfather replied. "We haven't seen that yet."

"Well, not *all* of it," Omar replied. "But we've seen a bunch of it."

"Nope," Omar's grandfather said. "Believe me, you'd know if you had seen it. The Capitol is a very impressive building."

"A building?" said Omar. "The capital has lots of buildings. It's a city."

"Oh! I see why you're confused," said Omar's grandfather. "Those words do sound the same! Washington, D.C., is our country's C-A-P-I-T-A-L city, with an *a*. It has a building called the C-A-P-I-T-O-L, with an *o*. The Capitol is the place where Congress meets."

Omar's grandfather opened his wallet and took out a $50 bill. He showed it to Omar.

"That's the Capitol, right there on the back of the bill," he said.

"Aha! I've seen pictures of that building before. It's famous," Omar said.

"It sure is. It's **iconic**," his grandfather answered. "And today it's getting a visit from us. It's fun to see the CAPITOL in the CAPITAL!"

-al versus -ol Endings

The letters -al in *capital* and -ol in *capitol* sound exactly the same when you say the words aloud. They are both pronounced "ull." These letter combinations are not always pronounced this way, but they often are. It can be very confusing!

All of the words on this list end in the "ull" sound. Choose the -al or -ol ending that correctly completes each word.

1. car ___
2. loc ___
3. cardin ___
4. petr ___
5. ment ___
6. glob ___
7. symb ___
8. pist ___

Spelling Words

vacation	vay-KAY-shuhn	*noun*	a trip taken for fun or relaxation
monument	MAHN-yoo-muhnt	*noun*	a building or statue that honors or celebrates a person or event
landmark	LAND-mahrk	*noun*	a notable or important site
capitol	KAP-i-tul	*noun*	a building where lawmakers meet
iconic	ahy-KAHN-ik	*adjective*	widely known and recognized

Answers: 1. carol, 2. local, 3. cardinal, 4. petrol, 5. mental, 6. global, 7. symbol, 8. pistol

Going Places with the
★ Scripps National Spelling Bee ★

Our spellers start their journey to Washington, D.C., for the national finals at the local level: in their classrooms. From there, they win a series of challenging competitions, conquering the pitfalls of English spelling and vocabulary at every turn.

In May, each speller takes a separate journey to the Scripps National Spelling Bee. Some fly over mountains, some cross lakes and rivers on vast bridges, and some hop on trains, while others take ferries and cabs. For some, such travel is uncharted territory, while others are seasoned globe-trotters. But by the time they reach Washington, D.C., for the national finals, no matter where they come from, they are united by a love of words. Our champion spellers bring their own knowledge of the English language and the regions they represent. We ask spellers what their favorite words are, and we like to imagine the places they were when they learned those words.

One speller learned his favorite word, *caballero*, while in the stands at his first rodeo in El Paso, Texas.

The charming *fennec* caught the eye of one speller while she was touring the National Zoo in Washington, D.C.

On a trip to Hawaii, one speller got a bargain on a shell necklace by using his favorite word, *hoomalimali*: the art of persuasion and flattery.

While panning for gold in the Gold Rush town of Columbia, California, one speller learned the refreshing powers and spelling tricks hidden in a cold bottle of *sarsaparilla*.

One speller learned her favorite word on a trip to North Carolina's Outer Banks when her mom told her the sandbar she was standing on was right next to a *lagoon*.

One speller had so much fun camping in a *yurt* in Wyoming that he begged his parents to set one up in his backyard.

And one speller found her favorite word, *tchotchke*, at the gift shop in Chicago's Willis Tower to commemorate losing her fear of heights.

All of these words, seen "in the wild," become linguistic mementos of the trips we take. And you never know: The words you collect on the road—or in your own home—may take you all the way to the Scripps National Spelling Bee someday.

The Journey to the
★ Scripps National Spelling Bee ★

Sacramento, CA

Vermillion, SD

Park City, UT

Durham, NC

Twin Falls, ID

Boston, MA

Nashville, TN

Index of Sidebars

Index of Spelling Words

Index of Spelling Words

Index of Spelling Words

Index of Spelling Words (cont'd.)

Photo Credits